Xylotheque

Xylotheque ESSAYS

Yelizaveta P. Renfro

UNIVERSITY OF NEW MEXICO PRESS • ALBUQUERQUE

Library of Congress Cataloging-in-Publication Data

Renfro, Yelizaveta P.
  [Essays. Selections]
  Xylotheque : essays / Yelizaveta P. Renfro. — First edition.
    pages cm
  ISBN 978-0-8263-5458-7 (paper : alk. paper) — ISBN 978-0-8263-5459-4 (electronic)
  I. Title.
  PS3618.E57626X95 2014
  813'.6—dc23
                              2013049534

All photographs courtesy of the author.

Definitions of "translation" and "to translate," in "Translation: Perevod,"
are compiled from the online edition of the *Oxford English Dictionary.*

For my children

Contents

Living at Tree Line

THE DEAD

I am at the cemetery, waiting for my nine o'clock appointment to arrive. The two women are thirty minutes late. The cemetery is peaceful in the chilly October morning. A squirrel digs with frantic speed in a pile of brown leaves; jays twitter politely in the evergreens; a fat groundhog snuffles at the earth around his hole. If I am very still I may see a timid deer emerge from the woods and bask in the sunshine among the old bone-white headstones, streaked with rust and black from a century of rains. My fingers, grown numb from the cold, are curled tightly around a manila folder containing my color-coded cemetery maps, which I designed on a computer using a spreadsheet program. I walk, kicking at the drifts of crackly, dead leaves, and read headstones.

Some people have expressed surprise over my choice of employment, but the truth is I like the dead. They do not make unreasonable demands; they are not stupid or mean; they are never late. They are quiet; they leave me alone. It is the living who try my patience.

I once worked as a crime reporter and had experience talking with the families of murder victims. That was one of the points on my resume that qualified me for this job at the cemetery. I knew about death, and I did not outwardly shrink from it.

TREES

I have always been interested in trees in a general way. I do not spend a lot of time looking at specific trees or learning how to tell an eastern white pine from a western white pine, but I like the idea of trees. There is something soothing about running your eyes over trees. Having grown up on the edge of a desert, I knew that forests of trees grew in particular climates and elevations. In order to see anything besides scrub and tumbleweeds or the neat, artificial rows of orange trees or palm trees planted by people, we had to go up several thousand feet into the mountains, where there were real pine forests, dazzlingly green and pungent. These were exotic to me. Palm trees and cacti were boring and dusty, so humdrum.

Driving up into the mountains, I always enjoyed watching the terrain change from the hard, thorny plants of the desert to greener chaparral shrubs and finally to trees. What I did not realize for many years was that there was an upper limit as well, an elevation beyond which trees would not grow—tree line. I discovered this phenomenon on a camping trip to the Sierra Nevadas, and ever since I have strived to get as high as possible, to reach the tree line and go beyond it, to breathe in the rare atmosphere of a place so pure that it does not welcome trees. It is desolate and rocky there, even more so than in the desert of my childhood. I have sought the tree line in nearly every western state I have visited—California, Arizona, New Mexico, Nevada, Montana, Colorado.

I strive for that breaking point, for the arid thin air of subalpine elevations, where the pines, spruces, and aspens gradually make way to bald rocks, where one crosses out of the vibrant land of the living into the barren land of the nonliving.

THE DEAD

The two women, who are selecting a space for their father, are very picky. They are Caribbean and Catholic and think that we bury people too close together. Each site, I tell them, is ten feet long and forty inches wide. They think their father needs more space, but they are unwilling to pay for it. They do not like any of the sites I have shown them. The first ones were too near the parkway. We have since moved away from the parkway. Now they say they don't want a site with dead grass. It is fall, I tell them, all the grass dies in the fall. It will grow again in the spring. They don't seem to be paying attention. They point to a large oak tree—the only tree of any size in this section—and they ask if there are any spaces available under the tree. No, I say, everyone asks that. Everyone wants to be under a tree. And I repeat what I've heard my boss, the cemetery manager, say: that tree won't be there forever.

I look at the two women—one is tall and wispy, the other is squat and round—and I think again that death is the greatest equalizer. We are not equal here on earth, no matter how many political philosophers or founding fathers argue to the contrary. Just look around, and you will see people who are taller, dumber, funnier, blonder, braver than others. But in death there are no distinctions; everyone who is dead is the same. Yet the living try to keep up those distinctions for the dead, by purchasing more ostentatious headstones, by decorating graves with more pinwheels and flower arrangements, to show that one dead person is more important and more loved than another. Does it matter to the dead? Does it affect them? The dead are absent and remote, like the place beyond tree line where the air is tenuous and there are no trees. Being dead is like the absence of trees.

TREES

The oldest living things on earth are trees called bristlecone pines. They live atop the arid mountains of the Great Basin across six western states from California to Colorado. A bristlecone pine can live to be more than four thousand years old. My brother and I learn this from a park ranger when we go on a walk among the bristlecone pines in Nevada.

The average lifespan of a bristlecone pine is about a thousand years; it is in rare cases that they reach four millennia. The oldest live at ten thousand to eleven thousand feet, at tree line, where nothing else can live. Adversity promotes long life. Their needles alone can live thirty or forty years; they are not wasteful trees.

Bristlecone pines grow extraordinarily slowly, their life processes stretched out over millennia. They increase in girth about one-hundredth of an inch per year. The ranger pointed to one tiny sapling, not more than a foot tall, and told us it was seventy or eighty years old. In two thousand years it might be ten or fifteen feet tall.

Bristlecone pines have exceptionally dense wood and high resin content, protecting them from decay. When they die, instead of rotting the trees are perfectly preserved in the arid climate. The wood erodes, like stone, from centuries of pelting winds and ice, and becomes sculpted and polished. A bristlecone pine can remain standing for hundreds of years after dying. Bristlecone deadwood has lain on the ground for up to nine thousand years, perfectly preserved. In this climate things are either preserved or desiccated—there is no in-between. After an hour in the cold summer wind my skin is chaffed raw.

I ask my brother, who is not a writer, to describe what a bristlecone pine looks like. He says one word: *mangled*. The trees are squat and distorted, like a candle that has melted down all over itself. Their blanched, bare, spiky branches point every which way; they appear tortured and somewhat grotesque, like the kind of trees one would expect to find in a Poe story. They are like pulled taffy, torqued into a contorted snarl; they are like a normal pine tree twisted in a fun-house mirror. Although they are not miniature, there is something dwarflike in their aspect; they resemble bonsai, except that a bonsai is a perfect dainty replica of a larger tree with everything to scale. The bristlecone, with its thick, clotted trunk and branches, is stout and gnarled, deformed, doleful. Yes, *mangled* is the word—like the twisted metal of a bad car wreck.

THE DEAD

When you buy a site at our cemetery, there is something included in the fees called "perpetual care," which implies that we will take care of your loved one's grave forever. It is a preposterous notion. Our earliest burials go back 170 years. How can we make the claim that our cemetery will always be there, that we will keep the grass on the graves neatly trimmed, that we will keep the headstones from tipping, barring nothing, including the fall of western civilization? No, we don't make that specific claim, but it seems implied in that vague, powerful word—*perpetual*. That's not quite true; if you read the fine print in our cemetery rules and regulations, you will come across the following statement: "Perpetual care does not include . . . damages from an act of God, thieves, vandals, explosions, unavoidable accidents, riots, war, or insurrections, or causes reasonably beyond the control of the Town." There is always a disclaimer, even in things eternal.

What makes the notion of perpetual care perhaps even more preposterous is the second word: *care*. The dead don't need our care. They ask for nothing, require nothing. Yet we spend thousands and even tens of thousands on satin-lined caskets and stainless-steel vaults and headstones of Everlasting Blue granite, to show we care. It is convenient to write off all of the care with one check. The price is quite reasonable, when you consider what you're getting for your money.

Is it that we did not care enough for them when they were living? I can understand this—right now I feel that I care more for all six thousand of our dead, including any cantankerous old tobacco-chewing bastards, than these two live women, who are still dissatisfied.

When the women finally select a site, which they will invariably do, they will ask me about headstones. I will repeat my boss's words—that they should take their time and not rush into anything, that they should be sure about what they want because the monument that they select will be there forever. I want to laugh when I hear this word. Did the headstone peddlers of 150 years ago promise the same thing when they sold those marble slabs in the old sections of our cemetery that the elements have since worn away, erasing all of the writing? The names and dates are gone; they are as smooth as blank slates. These new ones are better, my boss contends, these are made of granite, these will last. My boss is practical and doesn't think in cosmic terms. But I can't help thinking of a time when the forest has reclaimed our cemetery, when the stones have all upended and crumbled to bits. Look on your perpetual care and despair; your several hundred dollars sure didn't go as far as you hoped they would.

TREES

People have named many of the bristlecone pines. There is Methuselah, the oldest known living tree at some 4,700 years; there is the Patriarch, the largest bristlecone pine. Others have been given profound, charming names like Buddha, Socrates, and Prometheus. I wonder about this. The trees have lived so long without names, or perhaps with utterly different names. Will the names we give them today be forgotten a thousand years from now, even though the trees will live on? Perhaps if you live that long you have no need for a name. But we do, to label our brief flames of life and make each distinct and meaningful, and in the same fashion we name the things we see around us.

Bristlecone pines are not social trees and tend to grow quite far apart from one another. A solitary tree, standing on the outpost of a distant ridge, can be struck by lightning, catch fire, and recover, quietly living out its life and never bothering surrounding trees, which are too distant for the fire to reach. The ground is barren here; with no leaf debris fire could race along like a fuse. Each tree is on its own.

In the subalpine zone where bristlecone pines thrive, the summer often lasts just six weeks. During this time the tree must produce all of its yearly growth and store up reserves for the long winter. In temperate years the bristlecone pine grows in a normal manner, but in harsher years, when the tree has not received enough water or nutrients to support its full mass, the living foliage dies back until the moisture and nutrient requirements of the living parts of the tree match the supply the roots are able to provide. This process of dieback occurs whenever the tree suffers damage from any calamity: a fire, a storm, a drought.

This survival technique means that while a tree may appear to be nearly dead, with only a thin sliver of living tissue clinging to its gnarled trunk, the tree is in fact quite healthy. It is normal for a bristlecone pine to be both dead and alive simultaneously, sometimes more dead than alive, yet still unmistakably alive. What, then, is the distinction between life and death?

TIME

In the 1950s Dr. Edmund Schulman, a dendrochronologist, "discovered" the bristlecone pines. I wonder how many times prior to that they had been discovered. After making his finding, Dr. Schulman observed in "Longevity under Adversity in Conifers" that "the capacity of these trees to live so fantastically long may, when we come to understand it fully, perhaps serve as a guidepost on the road to the understanding of longevity in general."

In the 1960s, a doctoral student in geography doing research in the Southwest discovered a bristlecone pine that interested him. After receiving permission from the U.S. Forest Service, he cut down the tree. Prometheus, as the tree was called, was later determined to have been 4,950 years old. I wonder if this student, hastily pursuing a PhD, experienced a surge of exhilaration when he realized he had killed a thing five millennia old.

Drought, earthquake, flood, lightning, native tribes, fire, European explorers, corrosive winds, the bearers of Manifest Destiny, and ice could not kill it, but one graduate student did. I wonder if he finished his dissertation on schedule. Acts of thoughtlessness, not evil, do the most harm because of their proliferation; I've known few evil people, but many thoughtless ones. If nothing else, we human beings, with our swollen brains, should be required to think before we act. There is nothing else remarkable about us.

Methuselah, the oldest known remaining tree, is not marked to protect it from vandalism. Why would someone vandalize the oldest living thing? Because our own lives are so brief, and we have a need to make an impact upon this earth, however small, that will outlast Ozymandias's? I understand why someone would want to carve his initials in a tree like that. How many other things have been here for five thousand years, besides the rocks and the mountains and the earth itself?

The bristlecone pines are young against the backdrop of geologic time. The age of rocks and mountains and valleys is incomprehensible to us. The twisted lines in the trunk of a bristlecone look something like the geologic strata of the earth, curving, irregular. One can read the life of the planet, of a tree in those lines, just as one can read the life of a man in the lines of his face, his hands. Everything shows the marks of time.

For many years our cemetery was run by a group of what had become quite elderly volunteers, before the town took over its operation. Although the volunteers were rich in kindness and good intention, their record-keeping skills were haphazard, and I spend much of my time double-checking and correcting the old records. Sometimes, having exhausted all of the paper records and having made an inconclusive visual inspection, there is just no way to tell for sure whether a burial has occurred in a particular site. That is when my boss gets out a long metal rod, the official name of which I don't know (*grave probe* sounds too crass), and he plunges it deep into the ground above the suspected burial site. If the grave is occupied, the rod hits the top of a metal vault lid or concrete grave liner, making a distinct metal *thwump*.

Sometimes, however, if the grave is old enough, there is no distinct sound of thunking metal; there is nothing, no barrier between the earth and the dead. Back before the days of stainless-steel vaults, before we entombed our dead as if to preserve them for an eternity from the elements, people were buried in simple wooden boxes, which have long since rotted away. Sometimes there's just no way to know for certain whether a site is vacant or occupied without good old-fashioned digging. The strata have broken down, fallen apart; there is no distinction between the teeming black earth and the cold bones of the dead.

I wonder about people who are neither dead nor alive. It turns out that even among humans it is not so simple as two distinct categories, the living and the dead. We still have not agreed on what a life is, where to draw the line. Is life the beating of a heart, the firing of a synapse in a brain, the union of sperm and egg? Is it a life if it must be powered by a machine? Is it a life if the soul has vacated but the heart beats on?

A man called and told me he needed to arrange for the burial of his mother. Later in the conversation it became evident that she was not yet dead. I told him that this was a problem, that we did not schedule burials for people still living. *Oh, but she isn't,* he told me, *we're turning life support off next week. For all intents and purposes she's gone.* There is a woman I know whose daughter, killed at the age of nineteen by a drunk driver, is buried in our cemetery. The woman visits her daughter's grave twice a day, leaving offerings of teddy bears and letters. The last time I saw the woman she told me that her dead daughter had turned twenty-two the previous week. What does it mean to be dead, if the dead can have birthdays and receive mail? She will never be a day older than the day she died, I wanted to tell the woman, she is dead. But what did I really know about it?

Every human life is a flaring flash of light, intense and hot yet so brief, a supernova on a minute scale. We are not here for a very long time, and then we are here for a blip of a second, and then we are not here for a very long time. Why, then, does it seem to drag on so interminably at times, like now, with these women, who have finally, grudgingly selected the final resting place of their father? The mayfly lives for less than a day— does that brief afternoon feel like a whole eternity to the fly? The infant we buried last week lived only an hour—did that feel to him like forever? He was an hour in this world, and his parents will mourn him for a thousand or a hundred thousand times that. How do we quantify anything? What significance does time have?

There is something else about that baby who lived an hour. His maternal grandmother called me to make the arrangements. I asked her if she was familiar with our cemetery. *Oh yes,* she said, *I have four there.* Four? I asked. *Four babies,* she said, *four of my own babies are buried there.* And now the one who had lived had also lost one. Did she love the one that made it four times as much, for the lost ones? Did her grief at each loss multiply exponentially, or did it diminish, along with her hope of ever being a mother? What was it like to lose four babies, and now a grandbaby? I wanted to ask her, but I didn't. One does not ask such questions; they are unanswerable. I had learned that lesson as a crime reporter. The questions were difficult to ask, and the answers were unsatisfactory for everyone concerned—the mourner and the mourned, the reporter and the public. Words just don't cut it.

Still I wanted to ask her: Does the grief ease with time? How much time? Did she keep track of the babies over the years? Does she know how old each would be today? Are the babies alive in her mind, strong men and women? Meeting her in a grocery store one would never suspect that she had lost four babies; there is much more to know about people than what shows on the surface. They grow a thick membrane, enclosing each sorrow, containing it, cutting it off from the living parts; after enough sorrows if you were to slice the person open, you might see rings like in a tree, but with both a person and a tree you must destroy the thing to see its core.

TREES

How do we treat and interact with these ancient ones, the bristlecone pines? I don't know. What would we tell the mayfly? Carpe diem? Our time is cosmic to the mayfly, just as the tree's is cosmic to us. It's all relative. I only know that we would probably fall in supplication before a human as old as the bristlecone pine, before someone who could tell us so much about the history of the world. The trees could tell us much, in their more subtle tongue, if only we would learn how to listen. I imagine the same tree I see today, the puny eighty-year-old sapling, standing long, long after I am gone, and perhaps even after humans are gone—who knows? The tree, grown taller, twisted and gnarled, dead branches reaching convulsively in every direction, bears silent witness beneath a black, star-filled sky on an empty, rocky slope at the very edge of the tree line, at the very edge of time.

Soviet Trees

THE GIRLS CROWD around you, studying your face, your hair, especially your clothes. They scrutinize the words *Highland* and *Riverside* printed in goldenrod letters on your royal-blue sweat shirt. What do they mean? Are they a brand name? The girls demand answers. They ask you to repeat the words again and again. You've been taken captive by these anthropologists in the guise of Soviet teenage girls. Like all anthropologists, they see you projected through themselves. They don't understand why you would grow weary of saying the words—*Highland, Riverside, Highland, Riverside*—like some tired incantation. As far as you're concerned, whatever significance the words carry has been eked out on the third or fourth repetition, and you want to tell them that the words are now nonsense on your tongue, that you yourself have forgotten what they mean. *Highland. Riverside.* For the girl-anthropologists the words are redolent of freshly manufactured goods, and of freedom and dollars. They stare at your sweat shirt as though it provides a window into America, all of it, in its unimaginable wealth.

There a few things you need to know. It's the summer of 1987, and you're in Kuybyshev, a city closed to foreigners. The girls are Young Pioneers, and this is still the Soviet Union—but actually, there's no *still* about it. Remember that. It simply *is*, for you and the girls, for as long as you've been alive, and for as long as your parents have been alive. To say it is *still* the Soviet Union is like boarding the Titanic for her maiden voyage, looking out at her massive decks, and thinking, *Someday, I'll remember this as the time when the Titanic was still afloat.* How could you believe, standing on the deck, that either of those colossal ships, the Titanic or the Soviet Union, would ever go down?

You're only twelve—remember that, too—but you've been put in the oldest group, with girls who are mostly fourteen, because you're tall and precocious. They keep asking about what kinds of things you own, how much stuff costs in America, what the stores are like, and how much money your family has. They want a full inventory of America, from top to bottom, from side to side, as though America is just a vast storage unit full of material goods. You don't know where to begin, but you feel like a celebrity. For the first time in your life, you're popular, the star attraction. You suddenly have so many friends you can't remember their names. They crowd closer and closer, trying to lay their claims on you, trying to see what an American looks like. They comment on your American face, which leaves you stunned. Americans have always commented on your Russian face. It's turning out you look like no one at all. It's turning out that your amalgamation of Russian and American features has made you only uniquely yourself, unlike anyone else, which is the last thing you want. You're twelve, remember. You want to shout—*but I'm Russian like you!*—though quite clearly, you're not. Quite clearly, you don't belong here. The hot heavy press of the girls in the cramped humid room renders you an exotic cornered animal whose fate lies in the hands of your captors. And quite clearly, they haven't finished sizing you up yet. They haven't yet decided what to make of you.

They demand to know, among other things, how you got here. To get into the camp you have to have a pass, and in order to get a pass, you have to have connections. You explain that your mother was able to get you a pass through her former college roommate, who is connected to the trade union. The girls seem dubious. This is a camp for future Soviets. It certainly is not a camp for American girls, even American girls who don't believe they're American, who think they're Russian, which is the kind of American girl you are.

In your slightly awkward Russian, you tell your unlikely story: that your mother is Russian and your father American, that they met in graduate school in Leningrad, that you were born in Kuybyshev and lived there with your Russian grandparents and mother and aunt until you were three. And then you left with your mother to be with your American father in a fantastical place called Riverside, California. Yes, you've seen the Pacific Ocean. Yes, you have a river of sorts, but it's puny—often just a dry riverbed—compared to the Volga. Yes, that's the unlikely kind of rivers you have in America. And you have unlikely trees—palm and navel orange and avocado and eucalyptus—and unlikely stores, too, where, yes, it's true, you can buy just about anything you want, as long as you have money. Yes, Highland is the name of your school, but you don't know why. You know the names for many things in America but don't know why those are their names.

🜨

You share a room with five other girls: Tanya, Irina, Lena, Natasha, and Guzel.

Tanya is tall and skinny with high, firm breasts that are her pride. She's recently had abdominal surgery, she tells you, by way of explaining why she's lost weight. She informs Lena that her breasts are soft and far apart and low because she sleeps on her stomach and pushes them out of shape. One night when Natasha climbs up on the broad windowsill to look at the stars, Tanya tells her that lying on a cold, hard surface will prevent her from ever having children. She will catch a chill in her womb.

Irina is quieter than Tanya, with pale freckled skin. She spends her time staring into a pocket mirror, endlessly applying heavy eyeliner. From the beginning, Tanya and Irina are two of a kind. They want answers to the same questions. And they want to hold your stuff, all the time, your T-shirts, your jeans, your skirts, your hairbrush.

Lena is the one with a woman's body: wide hips, full breasts, a soft stomach. She's self-conscious and soft-spoken, and at nearly fifteen, the eldest. She listens to Tanya and Irina talk about your things and says nothing, her lips pressed together in a white line.

Natasha has a broad, grinning face and a thick ginger braid. She's good-tempered, a laugher, and seems to be a nature girl, not the dreaming-in-a-hammock variety but the harvesting-tomatoes-in-galoshes variety. She looks as though she spends a lot of time in the country on her family's dacha. At thirteen, she's the youngest, after you.

Delicate, thin-faced Guzel has a beautiful, long black braid down her back. She says almost nothing. She's a Tatar. You don't really know what this means, except that it makes the other girls dislike her. They whisper in the dark: *Tatars are no good, they aren't Russian, they're despicable.* Guzel, no doubt, hears everything, and that's the point. You hear, but you say nothing. You bide your time, waiting for some abomination in Guzel's character to manifest itself. You wait to learn the reasons why Tatars should be hated. You have a lot to learn.

🜨

Perhaps fifteen other girls live in the other rooms in your group. Many are like Tanya and Irina, bold and heavily made up, dressing in miniskirts and belts with large plastic buckles slung low on their waists. They go to the outdoor discotheque each night where the unfamiliar songs blaring from the speakers in the trees are often in English. You don't know how to dance and you don't like boys, but you go along because you have nothing else to do and you don't know how to resist the tidal force of the girls. They tease their hair to stand up in bird's-nest snarls and use hardened rocks of eyeliner that they soften with match flame and then apply with the bare wooden ends of matches, painting on broad swaths under their eyes that smudge during the course of the evening, making them look, before bed, dazed and bruised, as though they've just pummeled one another in rounds of endless brawling. They burn the hair off their legs with those same matches because they don't have razors. They've come to camp with boxes and boxes of kitchen matches, and the smell of sulphur hangs in the air.

Some of the girls are quiet and dress in shabby Soviet clothes. They don't go to the discotheque and don't approach you, perhaps because you're always surrounded by the bolder girls or because you're too strange, an inexplicable representative of evil America, like a fawn with a rocket launcher strapped to its back. The quiet girls shy away from you, and you know almost nothing about them. They disappear into the background, the trees. The boys leave you alone, too, unable to penetrate the thick carapace of confident, painted girls that surrounds you at all times. Tanya and Irina. Ella, Lyuda, Oksana, Rimma, Nadya, Vika. Their names will stay with you even when you retain little else.

❧

Several hundred kids are staying at the camp, ranging in age from seven to fifteen, housed in a handful of white concrete buildings, artfully spaced among trees, meandering paths connecting them. Each is three stories high with a dozen rooms per floor and a common area in the center separating the girls from the boys. Your group is on the third floor, and all the windows have been nailed shut. You hear a rumor that a Pioneer threw herself out of a third-floor window the previous session. You also hear about a girl who went off in the woods one night with a boy and came back the next morning with her breasts covered in hickeys.

Sergei Grigoryevich and Natalia Gennadievna are the counselors. Red nosed, balding, and perpetually holed up in his room, Sergei Grigoryevich seems profoundly uninterested in anything occurring at camp. He emerges only to slur out threats when there's trouble. Natalia Gennadievna is a chubby woman in her twenties who will be the only one smiling in the group photo taken at the end of the session, but you won't remember her smiling at all.

"We don't do that in America," you say, when Natalia Gennadievna chastises you for not making your bed in the morning. What you actually mean is that you've never seen a duvet cover before and can't figure out how to stuff the heavy woolen blanket back into it. But Natalia Gennadievna grows silent, and she never says anything about making your bed again. And so you don't make it. You readily adapt to slovenly ways. You're twelve, after all.

"We don't do that in America," you say again, when the counselors tell you to report to morning calisthenics. The other kids stretch and jump in a clearing to Soviet songs blaring out of the trees while you sleep in.

✻

Really, in one sense, it's all perfectly commonplace. Someone simply decided it was a good idea to put several hundred kids among the trees. And maybe it was, but so much stuff is hauled in from the city that the forest is hardly there at all. The three-story buildings, the outdoor discotheque, the hall with the grand piano, the full cafeteria where you line up three times a day: these distractions make it impossible to see the trees, except as long skinny poles to fill in the background, except as a white noise that's discernible only in the quietest, emptiest moments when you're bored to immobility, nearly, it seems, to extinction. The trees are just static to fill the silence, a meaningless pattern of sticks draped over the void. You don't give them any thought. They have pale brown trunks and green crowns. That's all you know. You languish equally under the trees, at the discotheque, in your bed.

"We don't do that in America," you say, when it's your group's turn to have kitchen duty. No, you don't cook food in America. No, you don't dish out food onto plates in America. No, you don't do dishes in America. You delight in your lies, in the skewed picture of America you're presenting. You gleefully concoct stories about precooked and prepackaged food, TV dinners, and dishwashers. No one, you say, does any sort of kitchen work whatsoever in America. You have better things to do than spoon up compote for the eternity of an entire day. You have better things to do than wash hundreds of plates by hand in foul-smelling dishwater. Eventually, you're put to work sorting the big aluminum soup spoons.

And yet, you crave adversity. You want to stand in line two hours to buy sausage or mayonnaise. You want to go to stores and look at the brown cakes of soap and jugs of vinegar on otherwise empty shelves. You want to watch the surly clerks tally your purchases on abacuses and then carry home fresh black bread in a mesh sack. You want to lug heavy sloshing pails of unpasteurized milk from the dairy store and haul it up the five flights of stairs to your grandparents' walk-up apartment. You want to sleep on a sagging fold-out cot, the metal cutting into your back through the thin mattress, with five people to a room—the same room that in the daytime serves as the living room and, when needed, the formal dining room. You want to scrub laundry by hand and hang it out on clotheslines stretched across the hall. You want to dodge the wet dripping laundry on your way to the kitchen. You want to watch the roaches skitter in the hall and bathroom when you turn on the light at night. You want more, even, than all of that, an adversity you cannot taste or imagine.

Getting up early and doing calisthenics and making your bed are not the kind of adversity you have in mind. Life at camp is not hard enough. There's no toil or suffering, nothing grueling and painful. You're all well fed and bored, indolent and full of teenage ennui. The girls are not the least bit interested in Soviet struggle. They want to dance all night in designer clothes. They want to lie awake whispering, badgering you with endless questions until you're answering questions in your sleep. *Riverside. Highland. Madonna. Kmart. Peanut butter. Pepsi. Disneyland.* You can't ever seem to get your own questions answered. For example, what exactly does it mean to be a Pioneer?

You hope that the first Pioneer meeting will give you a clue. The girls have come prepared with white blouses, navy skirts, and the ubiquitous red Pioneer scarf, symbols of their commitment to the cause. Your mother and grandmother have outfitted you with a similar blouse and skirt. For weeks they agonized over the key question: should you have your own Pioneer scarf? You are not, technically, a Pioneer. They don't want you to appear to be a hypocrite, to wear the scarf like a costume, like something you're pretending to be. The scarf can't be something you casually slip into, something you wear but don't mean, like an occasional wig, a blonde whimsically transforming herself into a brunette for the day. On the other hand, they don't want you to stand out and be different, the only one without the blazing red declaration at her throat.

❧

The girls take turns holding your package of American maxi pads. They ask you to get it out, again and again. They examine the soft plastic bag with the muted colors, the blues and lavenders and pinks, the swirling graphics of something vaguely wavelike, the reassuring soft-edged italic or cursive font, feminine and discreet, and the word that they probably memorize, the name from the West: Always or Stayfree or Kotex or Carefree? You're not even sure. But for them, these are cultural artifacts, representations of an entire way of life, a political system. They have to glean all meaning from a single sweat shirt, a package of feminine-care products. They study your things with such excruciating attention that you get the uncomfortable feeling that they now know more about you than you know about yourself. They are able to extract meaning where you see none.

They've come to camp with homemade maxi pads or with pouches of cotton and gauze that they fashion into maxi pads. You know about this: you've watched your grandmother sew your aunt's maxi pads on a treadle Singer sewing machine before coming to camp.

You give each of your roommates a maxi pad as a gift. They stay up late whispering in their beds, discussing what occasion they will save their pads for. Tanya says she will wear hers to a party. Natasha mentions the first day of school or a holiday. Lena says she might not ever wear hers. Guzel holds hers and says nothing; if she speaks a single word she risks unleashing the venomous hisses of *Tatar, Tatar, Tatar* from the other girls' lips, striking from every side in the darkness of the room.

The girls delicately handle the plastic pouches. They will be souvenirs from America, from this summer, to show other girls back home. *We met an American in camp*, they'll say. *Look, here's proof.* And they'll hold out the pouches, cupping them in their hands like delicate corsages.

Tanya and Irina look at your things, again and again, your skirts, your jacket, your nightshirt, holding them, fingering them longingly. They hold them so much that maybe they begin to imagine that they are already theirs.

❧

A counselor for one of the younger groups is a Tatar with a dour, pock-marked face. Somehow, he learns about you and befriends you. During afternoon rest time he begins to take you into the forest, to sit among the trees and read. You're not even sure how this happens. You have no way of explaining it to anyone. You hope no one ever asks you how this came about, and to prevent anyone from asking, you keep sneaking away with the counselor. Maybe in the beginning you just want a little break from the girls. Maybe that's why you go with him without questioning. In the end you won't even know his name. You won't be sure you ever knew it. If you did, it's conveniently slipped your mind. You begin to think that there's a lot about this summer that you'll forget. You begin to will the forgetting. Still, there are things that stay with you no matter how you scour your mind.

When the counselor takes you into the forest, he brings books in English and asks you to read them aloud. He listens in silent awe, soaking up your perfect American English. He's been taught British English by a nonnative speaker. Occasionally, he stops to ask a question about a word or to ask you to repeat a phrase. He wants to know about subtle differences in meaning and pronunciation, why the British say one thing and the Americans another, and you tell him: *I don't know. That's just what we say. That's just how we say it.* You merely repeat what you've heard. You're a recording of America. Push play, and you'll play back the tape. The girls don't even know what tapes are. They still listen to records. So then put the needle on the vinyl, and you will utter America, all of it, fluently, unthinkingly.

※

One afternoon the girls are languidly draped on their beds, refusing to dress for the Pioneer meeting until the last possible minute, when you pick up a stray Pioneer scarf and put it on your head, tying it under your chin like an old lady, a babushka. Natasha leaps off her bed, aghast. "You're not allowed to put that on your head!" she cries, as though you are desecrating a holy relic. When you quickly pull the scarf off your head, Natasha collapses back on the bed, laughing, as though it's all a joke. You feel miffed. Maybe it's true that you aren't supposed to put a Pioneer scarf on your head, but to break the rules is a gag, especially for you, since none of the rules apply if you're from America.

In the end, your mother and grandmother decide to send you to Pioneer Camp without a Pioneer scarf, and it doesn't matter. Either way, it doesn't matter. What do you even do at those Pioneer meetings? You can't say. Strangely, it's one of the things that doesn't stay with you. You remember standing outside in a circle while the counselors talk. You remember everyone singing, but you don't know the words. The girls stand with blank faces. Rather than being ardent or skeptical or defiant, they seem merely bored. They've done this same camp—or one like it—perhaps seven times before. For most, this is their last year. They need only to endure. They find nothing new or edifying in the same old songs. Some of them are even blatantly unenthusiastic, going through the motions with exaggerated boredom, like an American kid mumbling the Pledge of Allegiance with a wad of gum stuck in the corner of his mouth, intentionally slurring his words, his eyes trained not on the flag but on a comic book sticking out of his backpack. Only the girls' eyes are trained on your American shoes, no-name sneakers.

❧

The food is always the same, plentiful but tedious: kasha in the morning, then bread and soup and compote for lunch, potatoes with greasy fried fish or meat patties for dinner.

One day Natasha's family sends her a box of apples from their dacha. The two of you are the only ones in the room when it arrives. You both immediately fall on the box, gorging yourselves on the small, tart apples and laughing as you toss the cores into a corner. They make satisfying splatters on the walls and floor. The pile grows into a hill with a specific topography, and this core heap seems integral to your apple-eating project. The sticky streaks of juice on the wall, the brown gnawed-upon apple remains become your creation, not just a mess or a trash heap, but the physical manifestation of this experience. You are working as much to build this mountain as you are to fill your stomachs. You keep eating far beyond satiation in order to build the sculpture, to complete this work. You have eaten nearly the entire box when Sergei Grigoryevich appears, red faced and angry. He takes you out of the room and makes you stand in the common area. He paces back and forth, lecturing.

You've both stuffed your pockets full of apples before leaving the room. You reach into the deep pockets of your robe and feel them there. It's a Soviet robe, purchased right before camp, made of some cheap, shiny fabric with a greasy feel. It has a muted-green floral pattern, prominent green buttons, and enormous square pockets. Utterly shapeless, it's a robe for an old lady, a babushka, and you like it. No one else is interested in the robe. The girls believe you to be ignorant and oblivious, wearing such a robe, but you are perfectly aware that it's a dreadful Soviet old lady robe, and that's precisely why you wear it.

You and Natasha exchange a glance and grin. When Sergei Grigoryevich paces away, turning his back, you both yank out apples and cram them into your mouths, biting your way as far around the fruit as you can. When he begins to turn back, you drop the apple cores on the floor and stop chewing. He turns away, and you gnaw more apples. You find this uproariously funny and nearly choke on the apples, trying to suppress your laughter. Finally he stops, turns toward you, his face flushing red, and roars, "Who is still eating apples?"

He sends both of you back to your room to clean up the mess. Instead, you sit on your beds and stare at your creation, watching the brown oxidation slowly bloom across the apple-core landscape.

❧

Guzel grows more withdrawn. She's badgered mercilessly by Tanya and Irina. Tatars are good for nothing. They have awful black eyes and black hair and are not beautiful, blond, blue-eyed Slavs, the real pure Russians. They have no land; they live like animals. They take from the Russians. They belong nowhere on this earth. Go home, ugly despicable Tatar girl. You don't belong among us. Guzel takes all this in silently, and silently you watch.

The girls grill you about American fashion. *What do American girls wear? Jeans?* Yes, sometimes. *What brands?* You have no idea. You're not fashion conscious. You've just finished the sixth grade. Mentally, you're still in elementary school. You come from a small, mixed-grade gifted class. You come from smart kids, not cool kids. Your friends wear glasses and frumpy clothes. You compete by being smart, not fashionable.

You think Taz the Tasmanian Devil is cool. You own a red nightshirt with a picture of Taz and a big number 12 on it, which you received for your twelfth birthday six months before. You've brought it to camp, your favorite article of clothing. The girls eye your nightshirt. They're hungry for anything with graphics, writing, pictures, for anything that comes from somewhere else and has the mark of foreignness.

The girls ask about music. Before coming to Russia, you saved your money to buy a Walkman, and you own exactly one tape: Madonna's *True Blue*. The girls don't know what a Walkman is, and you struggle to describe it. You've heard of Duran Duran and Michael Jackson and the Beastie Boys. That's the extent of your music knowledge. Your parents listen to classical music. You take accordion lessons. The girls are not interested to hear this.

The girls want to know what you like. You tell them: Major League Baseball and Cabbage Patch Kids. They're miffed. What could these strange words possibly mean? You don't know any words in Russian that can describe your passions. You try to explain that your hero is a black man named Kirby Puckett who's good at swinging a stick and hitting a ball and that you want a team of men with sticks and balls from Minnesota to be the very best at swinging those sticks at those balls and to win the World Series. You try to explain the critical differences between Cabbage Patch Kids with yarn hair and those with corn-silk hair, the ones with cloth faces and the ones with plastic faces. You're not a good emissary of the West. Your explanations of life in America are sketchy, idiosyncratic. You've lived only in Riverside, California. You inform the girls that everyone in America has a car and lives in a single-family house, that orange trees and palm trees grow everywhere, and that it never snows. You are running out of things to tell them. And once they know everything, once your brain has been picked clean, then what?

❦

When Guzel silently packs up to leave not even halfway through the session, you want to apologize to her, but you don't know for what. It's the other girls—Tanya and Irina—who have driven her away. You've never said anything unkind to her. In fact, their meanness perplexes you. You've never been able to glimpse even a hint of what is so loathsome about her. She has a long black braid and dark eyes. That's all. Her Russian is fluent. She's a Pioneer. She was born here, like the rest of them, like you. And yet she's not one of them, so she must leave. She's quiet and resigned as she packs, as though this is an inevitable part of life, as though this has happened before and will happen again. You say nothing, and you justify your silence by reminding yourself that you're an outsider, too. Your position is tenuous. The girls can turn on you.

Shortly after Guzel's departure, Natasha begins to have stomach trouble. She explains that she's always had a bad stomach. You suspect there's more to it than that. She asks to be sent home. After she's gone, there are just four of you left in the room. You begin to see that Pioneer Camp is an endurance test that not everyone passes.

Every night you continue to go to the discotheque where you stand in the gloomy peripheries, in the sinister area between the flashing, blaring dance floor and the darkness and rustling quiet of the trees, in that weirdly lit middle ground between the writhing young bodies and the forest. You watch the others dance and wait for something more to happen.

❦

The Tatar counselor keeps coming for you and taking you into the forest to read to him. He sits closer and closer, leaning against your arm to see the text. You endure him there like a scorching sun burning your skin. When he leads you back to your room you feel elated, freed from his terrible masculine nearness. You rub away the sunburn sensation on your arm and think you cannot stand to go with him again. But you always do. One day, he puts his hot palm on your back and holds it there, and you continue reading in your perfect American English. He begins to stroke your back through your shirt, and you continue reading. You are very good at reading; you want to exhibit perfect composure. You tell yourself that this is a test, that you must read to the end of the page without a hitch in your voice. You tell yourself that this is merely one small thing, among many others, to be endured at Pioneer Camp. You tell yourself it isn't so bad.

And yet, when you reach the end of page, suddenly it seems that you've finished the assignment, completed your servitude here. Without saying a word, you throw the book aside, spring to your feet, and run away from him through the forest. You run all the way back to your room, even though he never even tries to pursue you. You throw yourself violently onto your unmade bed and announce to the girls that you never want to see that man again. They pounce on your bed, surrounding you, demanding to know what he's done. You refuse to say. With perfect composure, you repeat: *I never want to see that man again.* This fact alone stands in for all the others. You begin to see how your fierce insistence on this key idea to the exclusion of all other information could begin to color the truth, not just for others but in your own mind, so that over time your memory might be tidily compressed to a solitary statement—*there was a man I never wanted to see again*—a puzzling riddle of a bandage sealing over some damage you know better than to examine. In time, this will happen, or very nearly so. For now, you repeat your only explanation to the girls. *I never want to see that man again.*

When he comes for you the following day, the girls swarm on him. They block the doorway with their bodies, pressing together, pushing him out. They've become territorial, like vicious mother animals, protecting their young. *No, she's not going with you,* they say. *No, you cannot have her, our American. No, never come here again, you ugly despicable good-for-nothing Tatar.*

And he doesn't. *I never want to see that man again.* The girls grant you your wish. And still, you wait for something more.

❦

Then the sneezing begins. It is something that grips your body, a new phenomenon to be endured, one so commonplace that you can hardly bear the aggravation. *Once I sneezed all day long.* This is not even worth mentioning, when you later recount your sufferings, which makes it not even worth enduring. And yet it goes on and on. Late into the night you're still sneezing, your nose a swollen globule on your face. The girls whisper in their beds around you, the rough rustle of their voices just another irritant. Tanya grows annoyed with you. Perhaps her annoyance has been growing for days, weeks, over a host of petty infractions—your casual shirking of bed-making and calisthenics duties, your profound ignorance about fashion and music, your reluctance to part with your American goods despite your seeming indifference to them—until the late-night sneezing attack culminates into a full blossoming of her aggravation with you.

"Stop sneezing," she commands.

"I can't," you say, sneezing again as if to intentionally defy her.

Tanya leaps off her bed and marches out of the room in her nightgown. Several minutes pass in silence broken only by your sneezes. The girls await Tanya's wrath. Finally she returns, leading a tipsy Sergei Grigoryevich. She flips the light switch, washing you all in sudden brightness.

"She is sick," Tanya announces, pointing at you. "Take her to the *izolyator*. She might have some awful contagious American disease. She might infect everyone in the camp."

Sergei Grigoryevich regards you for a moment with hooded pink eyes as you sneeze.

"Get dressed," he finally barks, stepping out into the hall to wait.

Lena makes some weak protest on your behalf, and you see, for the first time, that she is your true friend. You recognize, as you slip into your clothes, that she has been quietly watching out for you. You want to remain with her, but you want to go out into the night, too.

Sergei Grigoryevich leads you lurchingly across the camp. You follow, walking the silent late-night grounds, past the dark discotheque, past the other sleeping buildings, and you notice for the first time the deep pocks of stars in the sky, and the quiet crepitation of the trees, and if you could keep walking forever you would not be afraid, but then he brings you too soon to another building. Coming in out of the night, into the hands of new strangers, awakens your fear. You have come to the izolyator, the infirmary, which to your ears sounds too close to the English word *isolator*, so you see yourself quarantined in a stark white room attended by doctors in full surgical gear. And this is not far from the truth. The doctors and nurses seem wary of you. They ask for your symptoms. You tell them a runny nose, that's all. They put you in a room by yourself and leave you alone for hours at a stretch, bringing meals and occasionally taking your temperature. You're under observation.

You find yourself in a white room with three white beds, but the other two are unoccupied. You decide to occupy them, because you have nothing else to do. You don't even have a window. You imagine yourself looking out a window, watching the sun pass across the sky, the girls passing back and forth on the paths headed to and from the cafeteria, the luridly pulsing lights of the discotheque, and the trees standing silently behind everything. You spend time in each of the beds, imagining looking out that nonexistent window and seeing nothing but trees. You play a game. Each time the nurse comes, she finds you in a different bed. The nurse seems annoyed, perhaps thinking of laundering the additional bedclothes. You find this funny but not so funny that you laugh. You have no idea what time it is, except that sometimes you are brought breakfast, sometimes dinner. You feel that by lying in each of the beds you exert your maximum impact on the room, that you have spread yourself out over everything.

In what you think might be the middle of the night, when you have been left alone for a long spell, you get out of bed and rest finally on the cold, hard floor. *Here I am, lying on the floor of the isolator,* you think. You imagine that you are in prison and have not even been given a blanket. You imagine it is winter. You imagine great suffering. You remain there for hours, a penance for something, the cold boring into your back, the chill no doubt invading your womb. If you never have children, that's just fine with you. The girls have cast you out, sent you to this prison. They're punishing you for something, perhaps just for being American. They're punishing you for something that's not your fault at all. Your sneezing has long since passed, but you don't ask about release. The girls put you here, and you will stay as long as necessary.

Finally the girls come for you. They tell you that you've been away only two days, but it seems longer, the empty hours stretching out elliptically in a white room with no time. Only your movement between the three beds and the floor has marked the passage of time. You understand now that the sense of time is created by external stimuli, by people and walks and meals, by the sun, by trees moving in the breeze, by clouds passing in the sky, by the frenzied beats of blaring music, by weather and seasons, by travel, by movement. You cannot tell any of this to the girls. You don't have words for it in any language.

The girls seem very much the same. They talk to the nurses and doctors and demand your release. They're a force to be reckoned with. She's no longer sick, no longer sneezing, the girls insist. Let her go. You assure the doctors that you feel just fine, and so the doctors release you. Outside the sudden onrush of colors and smells and the warm breeze on your skin makes you dizzy. The world has never been so stupefying. You can't believe the girls aren't stupefied; you can't even listen to what they are saying to you.

The following day, your head still brimming over with the world, you and Lena run away. And it seems that all that came before—the discotheque nights, the isolator, the endless questions—was only a prelude to this moment. Finally, what you have been waiting for happens.

❦

And it happens like this: one moment the two of you are walking along one of the paths, going from the cafeteria back to your room, and the next moment you've slipped off into the trees, and you're running through the forest, running away from camp, running with exuberance because finally your terrible slow languishing has come to an end. Finally you're doing something.

You don't know where you're going, but you have no fear of getting lost. Once you're well beyond the reach of camp, you slow to a walk. Even though you walk for a long time and see nothing but trees, you trust that you'll get somewhere. You trust the trees. You trust that they will not go on forever, which is perhaps a misplaced trust in a land as vast as Russia. Sometimes you talk, and sometimes you're silent. Later, you won't remember what you talk about. You're simply two friends among the trees. They're the kinds of trees with endless, straight trunks, with the branches interlacing into a canopy far overhead. You can't make out the individual leaves—or are they needles?—from the ground.

You don't know why Lena's here with you, but you have a sense that she's doing this for you, to give you something. You don't understand Lena. She doesn't ask you many questions, but she always listens to your answers to others' questions. She eyes your stuff but doesn't ask to hold it. Sometimes she hangs out with Tanya and Irina, and sometimes she withdraws from them. She is ambivalent. Her feelings about everything seem unnecessarily complex.

Walking through the spongy duff of the forest floor, you think about many things at once. Your thoughts explode, embryonic but powerful, not yet born into language. You understand that all summer you've been yearning for a transformation, and you wonder, if the transformation refuses to come, can the very yearning effect a transformation? Do you have that power? Can we make things happen to us, not just on the outside but on the inside? Can carrying your body away through the forest cause a revolution in your mind? You don't have words for many things. You don't know what to ask but feel that you are brimming with nascent questions.

You tell yourself the words you know. You're an American girl walking through a Soviet forest. You're a Soviet girl running through a Russian forest. No, these statements are too limiting. There is more. It goes deeper than labels, than senseless words like *Soviet* or *American. Highland. Riverside.* The wind rushing in your ears insists it's so. The trees insist it's so. You want to make so much more of this than it seems to be. You want this experience to take on the quality of myth. You want your likeness to be embroidered on a tapestry, etched in wood, set down in a book. You want this day to be deeply symbolic, pivotal, a turning point—or else you want for there to be a moral. You want at least to be a character in a tale larger than your own scrawny life. You want others to look on you running in the forest and to learn, or to be awed, or to be swept away—or at least to acknowledge or remember you. You don't want to be swallowed by time, pressed away in its folds. You don't want to forget or be forgotten. You want to live forever and for there to be meaning, everywhere, all the time. And you don't want the meaning to be in blue jeans or hamburgers. You realize that you want the meaning to be in the sky and the earth and the trees, in what preceded us, in what we recognize as home, more elemental than the name of a nation or a political system, in what we share in common—or should share in common—if we weren't surrounded by and distracted by and dazzled by *stuff.*

You are, simply, a girl running through a forest. You are fundamental. You stand for everything. Maybe it's the nineteenth century, maybe the Revolution of 1917 hasn't yet taken place, or maybe it's the new millennium and the Soviet Union is a great wrecked ship. That's how you feel, walking through trees. You've been lifted clear out of time.

And when you finally emerge from the trees, you see a village surrounded by open fields just across a highway—and it's the highway, not the wooden huts of the village, that seems the jarring anachronism in the landscape. You and Lena wait for a break in the cars, and then you run across to the village. You walk its dirt roads with no particular purpose, marveling at the wooden houses sunk deep in summer mud, at the crumbling gingerbread carved along the eaves, at the goats placidly munching in yards, at the wash hanging out to dry, at the horse languidly pulling a cart, at the ancient toothless man who totters past and grins and greets you, two girls from the city who somehow wandered into his village, his time.

You walk out of the village and into the fields, where you kneel among the neat rows of plants and eat the dusty sweet strawberries. You walk among tomatoes and eggplants, squash and peppers. And then you make a discovery.

"Round cucumbers!" you gasp, pointing. Lena kneels beside you and examines the beautiful dark green spheroid that seems to be bursting with such fecundity that it's ballooned into a miraculous shape. It seems a prehistoric cucumber, what cucumbers used to be, when they were engorged with the fullness of pure water and earth and simple living. Looking at that cucumber, you find yourself in the fields of the people who tamed nature, who invented agriculture, who first came out of the forest. You covet those cucumbers. You can't control yourselves; you work frantically, loading your pockets and hands with the heavy spheres.

Then you go back into to the forest.

❦

You return to camp late in the afternoon. You find Tanya and Irina chattering on their beds. They're only mildly curious about where you've been. You hold out your prizes and exclaim, "Round cucumbers!" Tanya and Irina seem momentarily stunned, and then they burst into laughter. They guffaw and roll on their beds, clutching their stomachs. "Round cucumbers!" they shriek. "Round cucumbers! Green watermelons, is more like it!"

You look down at the green spheres and instantly recognize them to be small, immature watermelons. Of course: how had you not seen it before? You've stolen armloads of unripe melons. Suddenly Lena bursts out laughing, which finally sets you to laughing as well, even though what you really feel like doing falls somewhere between laughing and crying. It's hilarious and marvelous and profoundly sad that two city girls, from two different continents, have made the same blunder. You collapse onto your unmade bed and laugh, but the laughter isn't genuine. It's only who you make yourself out to be on the outside, which now seems irrevocably separated from who you are on the inside, as though while in the forest this new rift opened up inside of you. And the inward-facing you has an equanimity that you've never before known and is far removed from the girls. It knows you will survive camp because it knows how to retreat, leaving the façade of the outward-facing you, which can cut all ties with the inward you, becoming just a container, an object in the world. *This*, you think, *is what it means to be an adult. This is what it means to survive.*

❦

In the end, it comes down to things: the things you have and the things they don't, the things you can get and the things they can't. They want to be branded. They want the words of the West emblazoned across their clothes, their minds: Levi's, adidas, GUESS, Nike, Reebok. They don't want generic, Soviet, socialist, communist. They want Things™, not just things. They don't want to be like everyone else. They think that owning these labels will make them distinct, of the West. They think everyone in the West wears designer clothes. Your clothes come mostly from Kmart or the thrift store or your American grandmother's sewing machine. Your sneakers and skirts are no particular brand. Your mother doesn't put any stake in labels. But to the girls, every article of clothing is a statement, and they can't figure out what your clothes are saying. What kind of generic American are you? Why do they know more about your country's brands than you do? You've never owned a pair of Levi's. You're not knowledgeable enough to distinguish that red wink on the rear pocket as a mark of class, of the West. They try to teach you, but you can't even feign interest.

No doubt they believe your indifference to things is characteristic of all Americans, when, in fact, its causes are specific: you're only twelve, and, ironically, you have a Russian mother who, being deprived of many material possessions for so much of her life, does not place great stock in them. There are different ways of dealing with scarcity. Some people, instead of wanting more, learn to desire less. Some people never buy a pair of Levi's, even when the stores are chock full of them.

You're twelve years old: this is key. You have yet to enter the penal colony that will be middle school, where everyone will dress alike in tattered, acid-washed denim with the requisite GUESS or Levi's labels, where daily you'll feel compelled to cement towering snarls into your hair with Aqua Net and obsess over the mysterious desires of teenage boys. If you were that girl—fourteen instead of twelve—you could provide the requested information. You would be an expert. But your Highland Elementary School sweat shirt really does say it all: that really is the extent of your world. The girls are correct to study it so long, though they misapprehend its significance.

Later you will seem to the girls to be an emissary not just from the West but from the future, from a time when the Soviet Union will be gone and the West will be ubiquitous. Perhaps then it will seem that if you were able to infiltrate their Pioneer Camp, surely the end was already in sight. And probably it is. But you can't see it, not in 1987. You all dangle your arms and legs and heads wearily off the beds, talking, trying to find a language to discuss things that you don't have in common. *I don't know*, you say, again and again. *I don't know what kinds of makeup the girls use. I don't know if brown eye shadow is in fashion. I don't know anything about dances.* Every day, every night, you persist in endless, circuitous conversations leading nowhere at all. But in the end, it's only the outward-looking you who's doing all this useless talking.

❧

Later, when you're home, the girls will write to you. And later still, you will seek facts, explanations, illumination in those letters. Tanya will write chatty letters about school, appending requests for jogging suits and other things before signing off as your good friend from camp. Guzel will write about her piano recitals, her plans to become a music teacher. Others will write, but it will be Lena's writing that draws you back, again and again. She will become the self-appointed conscience of the group, a witness to something that she considers a wrongdoing and that you consider nothing much at all.

Writing to you is Lena, with whom you picked "round cucumbers." Our school year has already begun, but I keep remembering how you and I lived together at camp. I visited Tanya, and she told me that they finally got out of you the things they wanted. I wonder what kind of impressions you are left with after camp? In the winter, she will write again. *I don't see the girls, and I don't want to see them. I am ashamed for them and for myself (begging you for things). Forgive us.* The following year, she will press on. *I am writing you a letter to which I hope to receive an answer. You are probably afraid that I am going to ask you for things, but that is not so. I am friends with people not for profit, but for the sake of friendship.* In one of her last letters, she will persist. *I simply don't respect them. I am very ashamed for them! To beg you for shirts, your jacket, your hairbrush, etc. I admit I also wanted to have the nice hairbrush, T-shirt, lip gloss, but I was uncomfortable acting that way. And when we were packing our suitcases, I already knew that Irina got the jacket out of you, and Tanya the shirts, but for some reason, I said nothing. I don't want you to be running around the stores in order to buy them "presents." I, too, don't need these presents; the most valuable present would be for you to count me among your best friends. (I give you my word that I will not mention this again.)* And she will keep her word. Your correspondence won't continue much longer. In the end, she simply won't be able to forget the things that are taken from you, and you will hardly remember them.

Yet you will study the letters until the words, written in Cyrillic script, will seem to disintegrate before your eyes, becoming like the lacy canopy of trees overhead, so distant, so indistinct, like white noise, like something you will never be sharp enough to decipher.

❦

So what is it that happens at the end of camp? You will return to this question, and the answer will always be the same: nothing. After you return with Lena from the forest, nothing happens. Everything has already happened. Your inward-looking self sits crouched deep in darkness. Outside in the world, Tanya and Irina want your stuff. No doubt they believe that you don't appreciate your things sufficiently, and so they deserve them more than you do. It's not that you begrudge them the things but that you want them to like you even if you weren't from America, even if you didn't give them gifts. And you suspect that if you give all your things away, you won't have friends anymore. So you hold on to your things, until the end. And then you give them away in a frenzied release, casting off possessions as though throwing them overboard from a sinking ship. It's the easiest way to survive, cultivating the saccharine niceness of girls who don't genuinely consider you a friend in the least, though there is much posturing, many declarations of undying devotion, because, after all, there is a chance they might receive packages from America, there is a chance that their American connection will come to something more. And it's only your outward-looking self that's involved here, shedding material possessions that are easily replaceable and that your inward-looking self has no use for anyway. How many things you give away, and to whom, you won't even be able to say. Tanya gets shirts. Irina gets your jacket, gray vinyl faux leather, probably from Kmart, probably purchased on special for $11.99. There's more, but a full tallying is pointless.

The only thing you can't part with is your Taz nightshirt, but this turns out to be a mistake. When you're packing up to leave, you discover that someone has stolen the nightshirt and the remainder of your maxi pads out of your suitcase. You tell no one at camp about this. You believe that you are being punished for your greed, your materialism. A true Soviet would not begrudge a comrade her Taz nightshirt, even if it's her last shirt, which it nearly is. Later, when you tell your mother about the theft, she'll promise to get you another nightshirt in America. It's as easy as heading down to Kmart. She'll dismiss the whole thing as no big deal. And, of course, it isn't. But the point is not that you've lost your favorite nightshirt but that it's been stolen from you. You gladly would have given it away to prevent one of your friends from becoming a thief.

※

The girls give you two gifts. The first is a yellow T-shirt with the red letters "CCCP" and a hammer-and-sickle insignia. You don't have any particular attraction to the shirt and simply pack it away in your suitcase, but later, in two or three years, that T-shirt, along with your black American motorcycle jacket with a CCCP patch on the arm, will become your personal brand, your countercultural statement, your growl of angst, shortly before the Soviet empire's hull finally explodes from the iceberg it's been silently scraping for so long. Seemingly overnight it will become cool to collect Soviet things. Suddenly Soviet will become retro, and the Soviet Union a funny little harmless party the Russians had for seven decades that got so rowdy they sometimes banged their shoes on the table, and the hammer-and-sickle insignia will seem quaint and olden, a nice historic thing to have around like an ancestor's butter churn or a flintlock pistol that no one would ever think to try to use again—but still, we hang on to these things out of a sense of history, out of nostalgia. But for now, the shirt, lying in the bottom of your nearly empty suitcase, means little to you.

Their final parting gift is a Pioneer scarf covered in their beautiful handwriting, listing the names and addresses and good wishes of everyone in your group. No doubt this careful inking is a desecration of the highest order. But it's also one of the only things they have to give, and surely it's a symbol of them as much as anything can be. It's a symbol not of who they really are but rather who you want them to be and perhaps who they themselves wish they could be, for your benefit. You cast away your American clothes and come home with a genuine Pioneer scarf. It's the one thing you can't get in America. Later, back home, you'll hold the scarf for long periods, thinking of your time at the camp, creating in your mind different girls, ardent Soviets who sing the praises of their country, who work happily digging potatoes or antitank ditches, who do hard manual labor just for the sake of doing work, who wear their Pioneer scarves every day from sheer joy and love of the motherland, who never give a thought to fashion and relish in the sacrifice of wearing shabby clothes, who embrace you and brainwash you into their way of life, their way of thinking, who declare you one of them, a part of the glorious Soviet Union, where people have ideals and don't put stock in material possessions. Holding your Pioneer scarf, you can imagine—and almost believe—that this is who they are. Touching their inked-on names and addresses, you can pretend that you are one of them, you have been taken into the fold, and you all have a future together.

❦

Later still, you will find yourself studying the few photos that were taken that summer, looking first at your clothes, and then at the girls' unsmiling frozen faces, and then, inevitably, your gaze will be drawn to the background, to the trees. You will squint hard at them, wishing you could see them more clearly, believing they have imparted some lesson to you that summer that you have yet fully to grasp. You'll wish that you could plunge into the photo and walk off among the trees just one more time. Your eyes will search the foliage for something that doesn't have a name, something that cannot be uttered in any language. You know so little about the trees. Their green canopies will seem like static to your untrained mind; you won't be able to make out the detail of their careful design, their patient unfurling and poise.

The photographs, finally, will not hold any more explanations than the letters or the fading ink on a Pioneer scarf. Still, a quarter of a century later, you will persist in seeking something in the indistinct images of those trees. You will feel the unending twinning of your selves, the inward- and outward-facing, and you will sense that in some wondrous way the trees can reunite the pieces of you that came apart that summer—because trees are singular, the full force of their strength and purpose invested in simultaneously reaching upward toward light, downward into earth, without any need for retreat or posturing, without contradiction. They hold their positions. The thing about trees is they don't have twin selves, and the lesson you take from being among them as a twelve-year-old, you will see, is not their lesson at all. The trees were never Soviet; they don't strain under the forces of language or identity. Finally, what the trees teach, what they mean, why they are crucial to who you are will still remain beyond your grasp, but you will continue reaching nonetheless.

Cause of Death

THE MAN WHO came to see me to buy a site to bury his wife looked like a man who'd been inexplicably slapped by the earth itself. He looked like a man who'd been knocked down by a colossal sea wave while standing in the middle of a cornfield. He looked like a blind, burrowing animal that had been spit out by the dirt and left to blink and burn in the glare of full sunlight. Actually, he didn't look all that different from many of the people I met while working at Chestnut Grove Cemetery, but I remember this man while I have forgotten many others. He was blindsided by grief, bewildered, as though he had been unexpectedly thrust on a stage beneath blinding lights and asked to play the role of a man who has just lost his wife. And he was still only figuring out how to be an actor, how to play this role, and it was vastly unfair that he didn't get acting lessons or at least a dress rehearsal. He was just in his forties—and his wife had been, too— and this was completely unexpected, he told me. It was just completely unexpected, he told me again. He repeated this phrase a number of times during our morning together, as though offering an explanation or even an apology for why he had not come sooner, had not prepared for this, had not filled out the paper work last week before this had happened to him and he could think more clearly. Completely unexpected: this was why he blinked his eyes so rapidly and seemed unable to concentrate fully on what I was explaining about the internment paper work. Yet he tried to be kind and attentive, decorous, as though he didn't want to be any trouble at all, as though he was there to please me. It was as though he was the one doing all the comforting and had come to make his wife's death easier on me, and not the other way around.

That same fall, but later, closer to winter, we had an ice storm. We sat in our house and looked out the window, wondering how our trees would fare. At first, it looked as though the trees had produced fantastical buds: the branches of the white pine and ash and river birch were crusted in miniscule white formations, like blossoms. Even the small dead redbud in the center of our front yard had bloomed in white, a young bride. The redbud's wood was mottled through with the passageways of borers, like Swiss cheese. Its branches no longer produced leaves, but every spring, a few rangy suckers sprouted from its trunk. We planned to remove the tree in the spring, cut it up for firewood, but for now, it shimmered in its ludicrous white blossoming, an imposter pretending to be alive.

We left the window for mere minutes—to gulp down our bowls of oatmeal—and when we returned, the trees had transformed. They were now encased in sheaths of ice, as though embedded in glass. The branches, frozen into thick, slick pipes, pulled away from the trunks; the white pine's branches reached for the ground, and the limbs of the ash bowed into heavy arcs, a fountain frozen in the act of shooting forth its weak jets. The river birch seemed exhausted. It rested its splaying multiple stems on the roof, on the ground. We didn't know how much weight they could take. As the moisture licked down over the branches, accumulating there, making the trees look heavy with dread, the gunshots started. That was my first thought when I heard the report of those sharp cracks, sounding at irregular intervals from yards in every direction. And then I heard a pistol shot in my own backyard, and when I looked, I saw that a small limb of the ash had snapped cleanly in half and now dangled by a thin thread of bark. The volley of limbs cracking continued all morning and into the afternoon.

᛭

The man agreed to take the first site I offered him. I even asked several times if he was sure, if he wouldn't maybe like to see a few more options, since no one ever took the very first offering, but he said no, this one was just fine. And actually, it was just fine, very much like all the other sites I could have offered, but most people spent a long time selecting, as though a few feet in one direction or another would have eternal spiritual ramifications, as though they were experts in cemetery fêng shui. But this man had no interest in the distance to the roadway or the view from here or the surrounding burials or the proximity of the nearest tree. I had picked a site that had another empty site beside it, and I asked him if he was interested in buying the second site for himself, because that's what we did at the cemetery: we thought ahead, and we helped our customers think ahead. But he just looked at me blankly, as though he couldn't possibly process any question that didn't have to do with *now*, as though I was trying to thrust him into yet another acting role for which he was utterly unprepared. I was asking him to think of himself dead, and he could barely comprehend that his wife was dead. It was too much. I told him the site would likely be there for a while, and he could think on it. I made a notation on the cemetery map, so that we wouldn't sell the other site right away. We weren't technically holding it for him, but merely giving him a little time. And I don't know if he ever came back to buy the site beside his wife. In fact, I never saw that man again, and I couldn't really tell you what he looked like besides having kind, bewildered eyes that blinked too much, and I can't tell you his name. But I have thought of him—and his wife—often, and of the time I spent with him that morning one fall.

᭡

My grandmother once told me a story about something that happened when her own children were in elementary school. One day, a mother she knew came to pick up her daughter from kindergarten, and the girl was so happy to see her mother that she came running toward her, beaming and lit up like the sun, but before reaching her mother, the girl tripped and fell and hit her head on the sidewalk and died. What was the cause of death? Blunt-force trauma? The sidewalk? Love for her mother? What, ultimately, made her die? I walked on the sidewalk where she died so many years before, and I wondered. I pictured the mother standing there with her arms outstretched, waiting for the girl who would never arrive, just standing and eternally holding out her arms.

᭡

In the late afternoon, after the moisture had finished wicking out of the sky onto the trees, we took a walk to survey the damage, to take stock of what we had lost and what our neighbors had lost. We were looking for carnage.

Our river birch lost three good-sized branches: they jutted out from the leaders, projecting a few feet skyward, then made abrupt, jagged turns downward, like compound fractures of bones, joined only by the thin glue of bark and ice. We paused and looked.

"God is trimming the branches for us," my husband joked.

"Why do they break?" I asked. "Because of the weight?"

"Because of the weight," he replied. "And because they're inflexible."

And while we stood there talking and looking, we heard a sound coming from a yard up the street, a ripping sound, tragic and prolonged, like something dense and overly ripe and doomed bursting open.

⚘

Four years before starting my job at the cemetery, I worked as a newspaper reporter. Once I wrote a story about a man who died when he drove his car into a concrete bridge abutment on the night of his graduation from the sheriff's academy. He had been tired from the celebrations and had simply fallen asleep, less than a mile from his home. He had not been drinking. He had finished the academy at the very top of his class. His instructor told me he was the "the most decent person you could ever hope to meet" and "a lovely human being." I drove out to the place where he died and stopped there on the side of the freeway to take pictures. The accident had occurred at two in the morning, and it was now perhaps noon, so there was not much to photograph: a few black streaks on the concrete, a candle, and several bouquets of flowers that shivered in the gusts from passing cars. What was his cause of death? Blunt-force trauma? A big hunk of concrete? Fatigue? Graduating from the sheriff's academy? Since there was virtually nothing to take pictures of—though I took them anyway, since I bothered to go to that place—the paper didn't run them. We did run a photo of the living man, a portrait of him in his sheriff's uniform smiling beside an American flag, but we did not run a picture of his cause of death. There was nothing to see.

⚘

That whole morning, I wanted to ask the man how his wife died. A car crash? A sudden illness? A heart attack? An embolism? A freak accident? Food poisoning? Suicide? A lightning strike? I knew it had probably not been foul play, because the body wasn't being held anywhere; the body was ready for burial, and she had only just died. I had no professional reason to ask the question, since there was no blank space on any of our paper work that asked for cause of death. It was my own curiosity that gnawed at me. And I saw that the man loved her very much. And I wanted to offer him comfort, but that was not my job, and that was not why he had come to me. He had a job to do here, and I had a job to do here, and we both did our jobs, and I think we did them well. And I think sometimes the most important things we can do are not part of our jobs, and so we often fail to do them. And so I did not say, "My heart goes out to you," which was a cliché but also felt like the literal truth. And I did say, "I'm sorry for your loss," which we always said and which always sounded insincere because we were a cemetery and we made money when people died, and if people stopped dying we would be out of business and I would no longer have a job. Perhaps the truth of the statement was in the word *your*—as in, I'm sorry for *your specific* loss, not for losses in general. We're happy to take the nameless, faceless, generic dead, but we are terribly, terribly sorry that *you personally* are in need of our services. And I wanted him to know that I was truly sorry, that I would much prefer that his wife be alive. I would much prefer to sit there with nothing to do, with hours to fine-tune the cemetery database. I would much prefer to be out of a job than filling out an internment authorization for *his wife*. But instead of risking saying too much, I said virtually nothing at all. Silently I filled out the paper work, trying to think of a way to slip in the question preying on my mind. How did she die? And more than once I cleared my throat to ask him.

✿

When I was in sixth grade and my brother in first, I went to his classroom to collect him after school. Normally I first collected our sister—who was in second grade—but for some reason on this day I picked him up first. When he saw me alone, he asked where our sister was. And that's when an alien thought flew into my head, a joke, a bit of random nonsense, a spoof, an experiment. It was exactly the sort of thing a child would say, and I was a child.

"She died," I said, without thinking. I really believe it was without thinking. At least I didn't think past uttering the words themselves. They were just words I said, and there was nothing past them, no future whatsoever, until I saw my brother's face blanch and pinch.

"Oh," he said in a level voice, and then after the briefest pause, he asked the question: "How did it happen?"

❧

The day of the ice storm, we walked through our Virginia neighborhood, looking for the source of the sound, and soon we found it. In the center of a yard lay an exploded river birch, rent completely apart by the weight of the ice, its branches splintered, its trunk cleaved open, revealing its mealy yellow core. We stood and stared at it in childlike astonishment. This was not our tree, but it could have been. The tree had torn itself open under the frozen weight of the water, revealing itself in its death, like a man sliced open with his guts spilling out, like something we should never see. And yet we looked and looked at the birch, the pieces of it blasted across the yard in chunks, the cleanness of its yellow heart shocking, even obscene, too private to be looked at.

❧

When Michael Jackson died, people clamored for an appropriate cause of death. Cardiac arrest was simply not acceptable, not enough. Finally, after weeks of testing, the coroner ruled his death a homicide. This was a better cause, a more explicable, fitting end for the King of Pop. We felt better, being able to point a finger at the cause of death. We can punish the cause of death. We can take his picture and put it in the paper and on the Internet. That will give us something to do. If the cause of death can wear a suit and appear in a courtroom, we can take action. This is one cause that won't get away.

❧

Outwardly, I was not bad at my job at the cemetery. I was professional and courteous. I was never overcome by the stories that people told, or, more often, hinted at obliquely. But inwardly, I always felt too horrified and curious. I was too much the voyeur driving past carnage on the road, looking at it through a crack in my fingers, as though the act of pretending to cover my eyes made up for the secret peek, as though as long as no one saw me peeking, the peeking didn't count. But it always counts. And what is that secret peek? What does it say? Thank God it's not me. I wonder what awaits me. I want to know what dangers to avoid. I want to protect myself. I want to see what terrible fates await human beings. I want to glimpse something meaningful and eternal. I want to see something human. I want to stare death in the face. I want to know if God exists. I want to know what's on the other side, and indeed, whether there is another side at all. All of this, probably, and more. I was first drawn to the job not because I was calm or indifferent in the face of death, but because, like others, I wanted to know more. I wanted to see death firsthand without being blindsided by its devastation. I wanted to drive by the carnage. I wanted a good view, a window seat.

✤

We stood and looked at the wrecked tree for a long time, saying nothing, thinking about trees, misfortune, and death, thinking about things we never voiced. And then we turned and walked home.

✤

When my grandmother died, the doctors didn't know what killed her. She was eighty-eight years old, which for the doctors was cause enough. They could not locate the exact cause of death. On her death certificate, they listed cardiopulmonary arrest as the immediate cause, followed by a host of contributing causes, including congestive heart failure, atrial fibrillation, probable cerebrovascular accident, sepsis, advanced age, and sick sinus syndrome. In the obituary that my aunt wrote, the cause of death was identified as complications from pneumonia, which is also true, since my grandmother's health went into decline following her battle with pneumonia the previous year. Her body was mottled from too many years of living; age bore into all her organs. And also, significantly, I think she decided she was done living. "I'm not going to make it," she told my mother in the hospital several days before she died. That statement was another cause of death. And if the doctors had bothered to cut her open and take her apart—which they didn't—they wouldn't have found a truer cause.

✤

The ice storm occurred a month or two after I met the man whose wife died. The man came to the cemetery in early fall, and it was nearly winter when the storm shattered the trees, but in my mind now the events are connected; my mind has erased or compacted all that came in between, so that the one event begins to stand for the other. The mind fashions such beautiful filigreed metaphors of memories, so it seems that an ice storm killed a man's wife, or that a man was wed to a gracious river birch, or that we buried a dead tree in our cemetery, or just that the sorrow of death can be made material, manifest, in a destroyed tree. The one thing begins to stand in for the other, so if I hear of a young widower, I might think of a broken tree, and if I see a cracked tree, I might think of human death, and I might not even know why, except that now those are the strange incongruous shadows those images cast of one another in my memory. They are both shadows of the same thing, and it is the thing itself I cannot look upon. I am like one of the prisoners in Plato's cave: I see only the shadows of things and take them for reality, truth.

❧

Now you don't even have to drive by motor vehicle accidents to see them. Photos of the carnage are just a mouse click away. I read an article about a girl who died in a car accident. This, in itself, is hardly remarkable. What is remarkable is that photos from the accident scene were leaked on the Internet, and now images of her splayed-open head have appeared on more than 1,600 websites. She is hardly a person at all anymore. She has become the Girl Who Drove Too Fast in Her Daddy's Porsche. She is What Happens to You if You Drive One Hundred Miles Per Hour. She is Terrible Car Wreck. She is merely Cause of Death. Her family, understandably, denies that this is who she is, and they are suing. For eighteen years she was a person, their daughter, and they think someone should pay for what she has become. But those images will never be gone from the Internet, or more crucially, the minds of those who saw them. And I admit that after I read the article about her family, I, too, sought out the images, so I could see Cause of Death exposed, cleaved open, baring all. The highway patrol officer told her father that she was "unidentifiable," and that was the truth: her head demolished, rendered past bone, to nothing, to death itself, past death even, to cause. And to see the photos is not to see the truth. To see the photos is not to understand anything. To see the photos is not really to see at all.

And I never did ask the man the question. I never learned how his wife died. And I still wonder. And I think, had I asked, he would have ungrudgingly given me the answer. Perhaps he would have been relieved to tell me. Perhaps it would have lifted a feather's weight of his shock. But in the end, I could not ask the question graciously, and I thought that I did not really have a right to know. I would not stop and gawk at the crushed body on the road. I would not search for the accident photo on the Internet. And I think, had I known the answer, it could never have been the complete answer. And I think, had I known the answer, it would have been like staring into the mealy yellow core of that blasted tree: a site too private, and ultimately, only a shadow of the truth.

Lithodendron

WE COME ON one of the coldest days of the year. A steady wind pierces our clothing, and the overcast sky, bruised a faint gray and yellow, threatens rain. We are kept company by a raven that sits on a lone post and period-ically rasps out a cry. The few other people who have come today are quiet and reverent, moving silently with heads bent to the wind. Wearing fleece jackets, windbreakers, and hiking boots, they move alone or in pairs. Our party of three seems excessive. There are no children besides my daughter, who is not quite five.

We have come to a forest that is a desert, a desert that is a forest. Vegetation maps identify this part of Arizona as "barren land" because greenery covers less than 5 percent of the surface. Shrubs, sparse grasses, lone stunted junipers, yucca, and prickly-pear cactuses stud the landscape here and there, but I have to seek them out. They are subtle, never accost-ing the eye. The Petrified Forest National Park is a land of barrenness: cracked mud, dust, clay, multihued strata. In places the landscape seems rusted, and this is not so far from the truth. Oxidation produces reds, pinks, oranges. In other places, the strata are blue, gray, black. This land of arroyos, washes, canyons, mesas, and plateaus has been sculpted by ero-sion, picked clean by time.

The eye does not at first recognize the trees in this forest. They litter the ground in great broken slabs like ancient columns that have fallen to ruin. They have been literally turned to stone: petrified. What is a stone tree? Is it mineral or vegetable? They rest in heaps upon the desert floor like great bones sucked dry by the centuries. For millennia they were pressed between the strata of the earth, like botanical specimens preserved in the pages of a book. They are long-embedded splinters that have been exuded by the earth's skin, which here is parched and scaly like a reptile's. Or they

45

are the blanched ribs of time itself, lying broken in an ascetic landscape. They are landmarks in time. The landscape itself seems broken, in a state of final ruin, and yet all landscapes are broken. All are in continuous states of creation and destruction. On this December day the land is just a single iteration of itself. It was never more complete. It was never fixed.

I stare into the bejeweled cross sections of trees older than dinosaurs, stained rust, purple, goldenrod, ocher, charcoal, lime, and white. I think I see cells and stars, microorganisms and galaxies, fish and pineapples, a hummingbird and a human heart, a starfish, a white moth, a CT scan of the brain. In some slices I see the face of a clock, hands frozen at half past twelve, at twenty past nine. The stone trees are like a Rorschach test of time; I look into these imprints and see not time itself but what it leaves behind.

🎋

For years a hunk of petrified wood sat in the yard near the garage at my grandparents' house in Riverside, California. As a child I knew that it came from a tree that had turned to stone, that somewhere there was an entire forest of such trees, and that my grandmother's father—my great-grandfather Herman Paul—had clandestinely taken the piece of wood. On one of his lone trips across the desert he had picked it up from a protected forest because, we assume, it struck his fancy. A gray stone with an incongruous texture that was, unmistakably, the grain of wood, it was the size of a large misshapen loaf of bread and weighed as much as a bowling ball, if not more. I couldn't lift it or even budge it. I imagined it to be a splinter gouged from the finger of a giant. A forest of stone trees sounded to me like a curse, like a biblical event, and I imagined that the man who went to this forest, this long-vanished Great-Grandfather Paul, may have in the end met a fate similar to the trees, and one day I might travel to the petrified forest myself and find him there, a man turned to stone.

Thirty years later, I am seeing the petrified forest with my brother and my daughter, who is about the age I was when I imagined a great-grandfather made of stone. The forest is more of a ruin than I could have predicted. The stone trees I envisioned as perfectly preserved standing statues, with intact limbs and possibly even stone leaves, present themselves as a wasteland of shattered monuments littering the desert floor. And yet, if my great-grandfather is anywhere, he is here, in this landscape. A nomad is not from any one place so much as he is from the places he passes through. My great-grandfather is of the desert; I know this. And I know that he found the petrified wood alluring enough to haul a hunk of it five hundred miles to his daughter's house. Though he has been absent my entire life, I have always felt his presence like a splinter, making itself known again and again, because in some ways he can never be gone. He was never put away, placed gently in the ground or in an urn. He simply vanished from the face of the earth. And so he tumbles up again and again, cast to stone in my mind in a hundred different final poses. In the photos I see him: the rakish rascal with the receding hairline, the diabolical rolling stone known affectionately as Herman the German. Yet these slices of time captured by a camera reveal simultaneously very much and very little.

I know him best through my grandmother, born Beatrice Paul, the younger of two daughters. I know her earliest memories of her life with him, that son of German immigrants who settled in Columbus, Ohio. I asked her for those memories so many times that they have nearly become my own.

Dad is driving the Model T, and Mother is worried that they will run out of gas. Polly is worried too, scrunched up in the back with Bea, but Bea trusts Dad. He's always right, or almost always. The journey seems endless. Dad is moving them again. They are always moving. There are always places where life will be better. Only once or twice have they run out of gas. Mother suggests they sing, and she begins "Button Up Your Overcoat." Bea and Polly join in. The song covers up Mother's nervousness. Finally Dad pulls into a Gilmore gas station. He takes Bea and Polly inside so each can pick out a sucker in the shape of a lion's head. Bea gets the purple grape one, her favorite. She could go with Dad to the end of the world.

To my daughter, born just over one hundred years after my great-grandfather, the fact of his existence seems as remote as the Triassic. She wants to study the deep past. She relishes skeletons, bones, old things, cemeteries, trees turned to rock. She has plans to be a paleontologist. Munching on a granola bar in the back seat of the rental car, she avidly watches the landscape sweep past. When we stop at Crystal Forest, a scrap of the shiny granola wrapper whips out of the car on the wind, and a raven immediately swoops down and takes it up in its beak. I recognize that greed for glint. People fill their pockets and cars with petrified wood, snatching at shine, at amazement.

Dad moves the family from Ohio to Florida where he opens a garage. Bea remembers only this: the morning she woke up to find the roof missing from the house, blank sky overhead. Dad puts her up on his shoulders and carries her into the street, where the water rises up to his chest. They look together upon the destruction the hurricane has wreaked. She is looking upon history. She feels this in her bones, even though she is only five. The year is 1926, and the news is bad. Dad's garage has been destroyed, and he has no insurance. They must return to Ohio. They must save again for a new life elsewhere.

What is it that is being stolen? What good is a hunk of petrified wood? There must be some good in it, because decades after my great-grandfather disappeared without a trace, his petrified wood still rests in my uncle's garden, where it was moved after my grandparents sold their house. And each month a ton of wood is stolen out of Petrified Forest National Park. This is not insignificant. This takes effort. These looters of history, of time, possess determination. They believe they are taking something of consequence.

Some have second thoughts about their crimes. The park receives numerous letters and packages. "Some years ago a friend and I visited your beautiful park," reads one letter. "While there I picked up a petrified rock as a souvenir. I have never felt right about having done that and now want to return the rock so that other park visitors can enjoy it as I did. I am sorry to have caused you this inconvenience but appreciate your returning the rock to the forest for me." One written in a child's hand simple reads, "Dear Petrified Forest, I'm sorry I took your rocks. Love, Meme."

Walking around the park, I begin to mentally compose my own letter.

Dear Petrified Forest:

I'm sorry I don't understand you. I look and look and I think about chess. I think of the knight, which is the only piece that can leave the board. Every other piece is anchored to the two-dimensional surface of the board. Only the transcendent knight may leap off the board, for an instant, into that third dimension. Looking at the petrified trees is like being the knight in a game of chess, like leaping off the board into the dimension of time to glimpse, for a moment, something more. This rain of metaphors I heap on you are my feeble attempts to understand something that is stone and tree, here and absent, present and ancient. These trees that are gone yet remain tell me that we are here and one day we will not be. Our understanding of not being here is like leaping off the chess board. These broken stone trees are like a skeleton of the past. The bones of the trees, pared by the wind, tumble and shift and shatter, though on this single December day they seem stationary, eternal. My mind picks over the bones, the rock trees. My mind puts them back together, and pulls them apart again.

And now, in a new pearly light, the trees are like broken chess pieces of the gods. We cannot know what their board looked like. We cannot know why they abandoned their game. For the Paiute of Utah, the petrified wood fragments were the broken arrow shafts discarded by the thunder god Shinuav. To the Navajo, the logs seemed to be the bones of Yietso, the giant killed by their ancestors. The Hopi call this the "place of departed spirits." I believe it is.

Dad moves the family to California. In Beverly Hills he gets work as a mechanic, working on the Cadillacs and LaSalles of the stars. Jean Harlow, Wallace Berry, and Clark Gable come into the garage, and they get down on the floor and shoot craps with the mechanics. Across the alley from the garage is Myrna Loy's house. She comes out to her back fence and talks and jokes with the mechanics.

Bea attends school with the niece of Boris Karloff. At a Hollywood pool she meets Mickey Rooney, who invites her to his birthday party. She turns him down. She has her reasons, including the fact that she doesn't care for boys at all. She's a tomboy. She likes to roller skate and run around outdoors. Polly's the one who stays home and helps Mother with housework.

Bea makes friends with a girl across the street. Together they collect pictures of food cut out of magazines. They are constantly looking for more magazines. They grow so desperate that they break into a neighbor's house to steal magazines. They're caught red-handed, coming out of the house with their loot. Dad is incensed. He beats Bea with his belt. He's a strict man and wants to raise his daughters right. He always says, "Don't do as I do; do as I tell you."

We stop at the visitor center to watch an educational video that somberly intones warnings about taking wood from the park, an offense punishable by fines and imprisonment. We learn that the area of the park called Crystal Forest, once a "glassy carpet of petrified wood fragments," has been virtually denuded by visitors. Time-elapsed photographs prove the point. The film also features an ominous reenactment depicting a tourist being handcuffed after a park official discovers a piece of petrified wood in his pocket.

After the film my daughter becomes absorbed with a panorama display that depicts two phytosaurs duking it out in a primordial swamp surrounded by a forest of coniferous trees. We learn that in the late Triassic, 225 million years ago, the desert of Arizona was a subtropical jungle of swamps and wetlands. Millions of years before dinosaurs dominated the earth, prehistoric Arizona was a land of fantastic creatures: cowturtles, gatorlizards, owliguanas, possumlizards, wolfcrocodiles. The phytosaurs, giant freshwater reptiles distantly related to modern crocodiles and alligators, reached up to thirty feet in length.

No birdsong could be heard in the mighty forests of this pre-avian world. Many of the trees that grew here—and that would one day make the unlikely journey through time to become petrified—were straight-trunked conifers, *Araucarioxylon arizonicum*. On average they were eighty to one hundred feet tall, three to four feet in diameter, but some may have grown to two hundred feet in height and ten feet in trunk diameter. I imagine their violent histories, their long travels that left them lying at my feet on a windswept desert floor. Growing near the banks of rivers, these trees were torn loose by torrents from sudden floods and were tumbled down the river, their bark and branches and roots shorn off along the way, their trunks abraded, bashed, and battered, until they came to rest in the bottoms of lagoons and swamps where they were buried in sand, silt, and volcanic ash, being in effect sealed off, preserved from decay.

Under these conditions, the process of petrification did its slow work, the silica seeping into the pores of the wood, minerals replacing cellulose, crystallizing into pockets of quartz, jasper, amethyst. The organic was rendered mineral, a much heavier and harder and enduring incarnation. It is not the thing it used to be, yet it has its form. The damage of living is also preserved in petrification. Fungus pockets, insect borings, and scars from the tree's life are written in stone. For millions of years the stone trees remained buried in the earth until geologic forces thrust them out into view.

These broken stained teeth of time are harder than steel but so brittle that they easily shatter. I look upon them as but one part of the vanished creature known as the Triassic, and I cannot in my mind reconstruct from these bones the full creature, the whole teeming landscape that was here. My task is akin to reconstructing an ancient shark from its fossilized teeth, often the only part of its cartilaginous skeleton that survives. I am reduced to reconstructing time from trees turned to stone. I still cannot answer even the most basic questions. For example, is it more tree, or more rock? My mind is petrified by the duality. I think of its short life as a tree, of the insects that bored into it, of the animals that ate its cones or bark. I am just another creature, taking something from the tree. Even by only looking, I am taking.

Dad moves the family again and again. Near Victorville they homestead in a shack in the desert on about twenty acres. In order to take possession of the land after five years, they're required to make certain improvements, including clearing a section of the land and drilling a well. Bea and Polly help with the well. Dad digs a deep hole and then gets down into it to fill buckets with dirt. Meanwhile, the girls stand at the top and operate a crank that raises the bucket. They empty out the dirt and then lower the bucket. They work at this all day in the heat of the desert, going deeper and deeper, but they never hit water.

Unable to drill a functioning well, Dad decides to abandon the homestead. They all move to a neighbor's house. Dad gets his old job back so that they can get back on their feet. He comes home on weekends. The school is twelve miles away in Adelanto. To get to school, the girls must travel in a Model T over a narrow, dirt road. Polly refuses to drive, so Dad makes Bea responsible for driving both of them to school each morning. Bea is twelve years old.

In the parking area at Jasper Forest, my brother and I get out of the car and in a moment of minor miscommunication throw open both rear doors for my daughter in the back seat. Suddenly, a fierce gust blows through the rear of the car as through a wind tunnel, bringing a dog of some sort with it. The dog, a brindled squirming mass, bounds across the back seat, over my startled daughter's lap, and passes out the other open door, emerging on the other side of the car. Its Gore-Tex-clad owner rushes over to apologize and to take the miscreant animal in hand. Faint dusty dog prints mar the upholstery in the Ford Focus and the fabric of my daughter's pants, but quickly her initial surprise turns into delight.

As we walk among the wood at Jasper Forest, her mind is filled with images of the dog. Later, in the retelling and the reshaping, this episode becomes a high point of the trip for her: the dog that was looking at petrified wood and passed through our car as through a burrow to another place. This roving dog becomes part of her narrative about stone trees. Like all of us, she finds meaning wherever she can. The petrified wood now has meaning too; it is important, uniquely hers. Later, she will find it at the San Bernardino County Museum in California, at the Children's Museum in West Hartford, Connecticut, and at the Henry Doorly Zoo in Omaha, Nebraska. Her eyes have been opened to it. Her world is full of it.

When Dad is unemployed, the family receives clothes and food through a WPA program. It's the Depression. They don't have meat often, and sometimes Bea misses it so much she goes out in the desert, finds a turtle, and throws it into a pot for turtle soup. When she's craving chicken she takes her shotgun, shoots sparrows off the wires, and fries them.

Dad decides to raise a prize pig. He spends so much money to fatten it up that the pig eats better than the family. He's promised that once it's full grown they'll have delicious pork, but when it comes time to slaughter it, Dad sells it instead. "I have too much invested in that pig," he says.

Dad often takes the family to the beach at Palos Verdes, where he dives underwater to pry abalone off the rocks for dinner. Once an abalone shell closes on his hand and he nearly can't pry it open. He and Mother go out to some rocks far from the shore and fish while Polly and Bea watch from the beach. The waves come in and slam against the rocks, and Bea fears her parents will be carried away. Once Mother is knocked off her feet and swept away by a powerful wave. Bea watches as she is bashed against the rocks. When she pulls herself from the water, her shoulder is badly cut. After that, Mother never goes out on the rocks again, and Dad fishes alone.

Human history, too, is written in the park. The ancient Puebloans left their mark here in the pictograms they chiseled and pounded into stone, in the ruins of their dwellings, in their solar calendars. Much later, the Spanish explorers came through. In 1540 Francisco Vázquez de Coronado stopped long enough to give this desert a name: el Desierto Pintado. To this day, we call part of this landscape the Painted Desert. In 1853 Amiel Weeks Whipple discovered a creek full of stone trees. He called it Lithodendron Wash. In the late 1800s the railroad came through, followed in the early twentieth century by highways. Wood began leaving the park in large quantities, even though the area has been protected since 1906 as a national monument and since 1962 as a national park.

Standing here, I see a landscape similar to the one the ancient people looked over, a landscape of Coronado's time and of Whipple's. I see a landscape of the 1950s, when my great-grandfather may have passed through here, chucking a hunk of petrified wood into his car, which was probably low on gas. We were all here, looking at these ruins. It means something that we still share this landscape in common, that I can stand here and see what others saw before me, while much of the rest of the world would be unrecognizable to my forebears. It means something that we have chosen to preserve this monument to time.

Yet this is a mutable place. The landscape changes. We try to stop it, to introduce stasis. At Agate Bridge we witness these human efforts. This natural bridge, a petrified log spanning over one hundred feet across an arroyo, has been reinforced with concrete to prevent—or rather delay—its collapse. In the end nature always has its way, but nature is interminably slow. Breathlessly we wait for the earth to churn up more treasures. We are impatient for nature to do its work, and simultaneously we want to cast it in a museum case, freeze it forever. We do not know what we want. We keep on wanting it nonetheless.

When first Polly and then Bea turn eighteen and graduate from high school, Dad kicks them out of the house. His duty is done. Bea heads to Riverside and gets a job as a carhop at Ruby's Drive-In. Some nights she cruises with the cops who come in at the end of her late shift. She goes out with a singer. One day a suitor named Bob Renfro begins hanging around. Bea's parents, still on the move, are now in Las Vegas. Bob offers to drive her to Vegas to visit them, and she agrees because a ride in a car beats taking the bus. Bob pesters her the whole way about getting married, and she gets so fed up that she agrees just so that he'll leave her alone. After getting married at a Las Vegas wedding chapel, they head back to Riverside. Bea tries to resume her life, working at the drive-in, cruising with cops. She doesn't want to be married and refuses to have anything to do with Bob. When Dad gets wind of what Bea's doing, he comes down from Vegas and makes her go with Bob. He tells her that she must obey her husband. She's always obeyed Dad, so she goes with Bob. Forever after, she goes with Bob. She's made her bed, and now she must lie in it. Dad's duty to his family is done.

Some of the petrified logs rest high on ridges. They have created their own pedestals, shielding the earth and clay on which they rest from erosion while the surrounding land gets eaten away by rain and wind. But nature will hold the log on its pedestal for only so long, eventually dropping it to tumble down the mesa slope to sudden destruction. These logs seem permanent, fixed, yet their eventual tumbling seems inevitable. They will roll and be dashed apart, and others waiting nascent beneath the surface of the earth will emerge.

As we walk I pick up small pieces of petrified wood and drop them. I am too timid or respectful to take the wood. I cannot swipe time. I cannot take what is not mine. Or maybe the educational video has had its intended effect and I am afraid of being caught. Or perhaps I am kept honest by the vigilance of my daughter. She has earned a "junior ranger" badge after being indoctrinated by the park rangers, who grill her on the proper action to take if she sees anyone taking wood from the park. She passes the test. She has learned to "protect the petrified wood *for* each and every one of us and *from* each and every one of us." We are all potential thieves.

A fraction of the billions of trees living today are gems of the distant future. The odds of petrification, I learn, are not even one in a million. Still, those odds are better than the odds of winning the lottery. If I look at enough trees, I will see a future stone tree in its living organic incarnation. This seems important, too.

Bea names her firstborn Paul. When the baby's five months old, Dad comes to see him. She's a twenty-one-year-old new mother, nervous about the visit. Dad begins drinking and becomes too rough with Paul. He frightens the baby by tossing him up in the air. Bea tells Dad to stop because he's making Paul cry. Dad grows angry and says she's teaching Paul to be a sissy. Bea stands up to him, telling him Paul is too little for such rough treatment. Dad leaves in a rage. She calls out to him and asks him to stay until Bob comes home from work, but he gets in his car and speeds away. It's just getting dark and beginning to drizzle. He's driving too fast with poor visibility, and he's been drinking. Out of the semidarkness a man steps right in the path of Dad's car. The man is killed. Dad is arrested and sentenced to a year in jail.

Instead of stealing time, I decide to buy it from the park's gift shop. I spend half an hour perusing the selection of petrified wood specimens, all obtained legally from private land, all with hefty price tags. My brother and I show one another choice pieces, disagreeing on which is the best. We have different standards. What am I looking for? I cannot say. I'll know it when I see it. I finally settle on a piece priced at $24. My brother concedes that my choice is pretty good but not the best. He doesn't buy his choice. He doesn't need to buy time. My piece of legally obtained petrified wood has pleasing but not garish colors: muted blue and rust with slender black and white veins, and equally important, evidence of its grain, of its previous treeness. It is, I imagine, about the size of my heart.

Later, it will sit on my desk, a two-pound chunk of time, an anchor to the past. Still later, I will move it 1,300 miles when we relocate. It travels far from its source, both in terms of place and time. My packing and moving it—this tumbling about in boxes of pens and paper and paper clips—is just another form of the ceaseless tumbling of the earth. I am just another organism of the earth exerting forces on it. My coveting of it is not unique. My hoarding of it will not save it.

❧

I keep insisting these trees mean something. I keep insisting a great-grandfather I never saw has something to do with me. To see this wood, I think, is to know the man. This was the landscape of his soul. This was the kind of place he sought his whole life. Trying to know the man is like staring at the ancient logs and trying to reconstruct a tree—let alone a whole landscape, a time—out of them. He has been a splinter buried in my imagination all these years. His piece of petrified wood is as much a final monument, a headstone, as he will ever have, and he selected it himself. He has vanished into a fold of time. Maybe someday time will spit him back out, a stone torso or a leg tumbled down to the present. What would I do finding such a curiosity resting at my feet?

Over the decades his likeness has washed away, to be replaced by the glinting gems of stories. His flesh is gone, replaced by words. I never knew the man, the flesh. I can only collect the stories, the words, and assemble them into something that almost resembles a man but is made of nothing organic, with none of the parts that make up most men. I replace him, bit by bit, until he is made of words.

Bea's parents divorce, and Mother comes to live with Bea and Bob and their growing family. Dad continues drifting from place to place, but he keeps a trailer on the Renfro property. His visits never last long. He begins making regular trips to Mexico. He takes down carloads of thrift store clothes and trades them for lobsters. He's still trying to make a buck, trying to get ahead, trying to find that place where the grass is greener. During one of his desert wanderings, he picks up the chunk of petrified wood, just another piece of detritus from a roving life, and leaves it at his daughter's house. Perhaps he has plans for it. Perhaps his plan has already been realized: simply to move it and call it his own, to place it at his daughter's home. No one, it seems, gives it another thought.

Bea and Bob eventually have six children. After all that moving in her childhood, Bea is content to stay put. She spends the rest of her life in Riverside.

I have been known to drive around with no gas in the tank. I can always make it a little farther. And in the last decade, my husband and I have owned six houses in four different states. Counting temporary rental arrangements, we have averaged one move a year for ten years. I believe that I hardly think of the stone man, but I must. I must seek myself in him, or him in myself. I have made a thousand-mile pilgrimage to look at stone trees. I am seeking something.

Though he was my father's mother's father, I carry his last name embedded within my middle name because in a twist of fate I was born in the Soviet Union where my father's first name was passed to me via the Russian patronymic system. I am Paulovna, daughter of Paul.

He has always been gone to me. When did he vanish for the others? When did they decide he was never coming back? No one can tell me with any certainty. If he were alive today, he would be over one hundred. I imagine him living out his last days in a Florida mobile home park. He could be anywhere.

❋

We walk and walk and look and look, until our bodies are numb from cold and our minds numb from saturation. We have taken in as much as we can. We eat hot Mexican food and head back to the motel, where we watch a college football game, even though none of us likes football. Chaffed and chilled to the bone, we shiver under the thin motel blankets, warming ourselves from the day of blasting wind. Texas beats Nebraska, my current adopted state, 13–12.

Bea's story has an end, but Dad's doesn't. There is no way to satisfactorily conclude his narrative. Bea told his story many times in many different ways. In her last telling, shortly before her death at age eighty-eight, the story ends like this: Dad has two close calls on his trips to Mexico. Once his boat capsizes in the ocean, and he floats holding on to a piece of driftwood for hours. Just as his strength is giving out and he's about to let go, a boat comes along and saves him. Another time, he's stranded in the desert without any water, and as he staggers along, his tongue so swollen from thirst that he can't close his mouth, some people come along and give him water. The third time, however, he's not so lucky. One day he goes off on one of his trips to Mexico and never returns.

Was his roving heart always seeking home and never finding it? Is home in the flashing of scenery outside a car window, in the pavement rolling under tires, in making it always to the next gas station, in the desert unfurling along lonely highways? Is home the American dream, which isn't a place but rather a promise that things will be better right over the next rise, that the grass will always be greener elsewhere? Home is in a piece of petrified wood you can take with you; home is in the stark landscape of the desert, a place you only pass through. Home is not the place you stay but the places that stay with you. Home is glimpsing yourself in time. These badlands of Arizona, too, are my home. In the American tradition, I pick up home wherever I find it, a conglomerate of the places I've been, sometimes stolen, sometimes bought, but always coming at a price.

In the morning we drive back to Albuquerque and board a plane. In my luggage is my own petrified wood, my own piece of time, of home.

Translation: Perevod

Riverside, California
February, 2001

I had known for a long time that the letters existed, and that someday they would be mine. I had seen glimpses of them, when my mother took them off the shelf in her closet to seek an answer to one of my questions. What was my first word? When did I walk? What other names did she think about calling me? She would leaf through the letters until she found the answer, and then put them back. I knew they were my birthright—part of my story, as well as hers—but I did not know when they might become mine. I thought perhaps when my parents were very old, or even gone. I did not expect my mother to offer them to me when I was twenty-six, newly married.

"The letters are here, whenever you want them," she said to me in Russian. "If you don't have room for them this time, you can take them next time."

"I'll take them this time," I replied in English.

I was sitting at the table in my parents' living room. My mother stood in the doorway to the kitchen; without saying another word, she turned and walked to her bedroom.

"Here they are," she said, returning with the stack of letters, a foot high. "Now you can write a book."

"Do you have something to put them in?" I asked. We continued to speak in different languages.

She set the letters down on the table and again left the room. Through the sliding glass door I could see the cement patio and beyond it, the rain splattering bare patches of earth in the backyard. This was my first visit home since I had married and moved from Southern California to

Virginia seven months before. Although I had not lived with my parents for six years, I had never been more than a thirty-minute drive away.

My mother returned with a duffel bag and began packing the letters. As she zipped the bag closed and handed it to me, we did not speak. We do not speak a lot, and there is a lot we do not speak about.

Back in Virginia, I unpacked the bag, handling the letters cautiously. I looked through them, reading dates, feeling the paper, studying the loops and jags of my parents' handwriting. The first letter, written by my mother, was dated June 9, 1974. The correspondence ended four years later, in June of 1978. I noticed that the letters were written in a mixture of Russian and English. I looked at my father's orderly handwriting, covering the front and back of hundreds of sheets of lined loose-leaf paper, the kind that schoolchildren use. I looked at my mother's more uneven, impetuous scroll, written in a dozen different inks on scraps of paper of various sizes, colors, textures: graph paper, tissue paper, squares torn out of notebooks, grainy newsprint. My father tended to remain committed to one language or the other in his letters, while my mother switched back and forth errat-ically, sometimes in the middle of sentences. I found a Western Union telegram to my father, announcing my birth. I looked at a kidney-shaped tracing of my foot. I looked at the drawing of an elephant that I did at the age of three.

One section of a letter written by my mother, dated September 23, 1977, caught my eye. It was composed when my parents had been apart for more than three years. In Russian, she wrote:

> *I want to write that it is again autumn. And once again without you. The rain makes the old leaves fragrant. The apples on our balcony are getting wet, and a cold wind blows. For me this is the most vigorous time. And my thoughts, coming with astonishing speed, make the dry matter of words banal. My last autumn in Russia. And the feeling is entirely of a lived life. And tiredness. If only I could see you and your eyes for an instant, every-thing would pass—this dry melancholy and the enormous feeling of the loss of something native. . . . My love, my passion and sadness do not give me peace day or night. I don't know what is wrong with me—it seems that this is the weather of rhythmic prose. But into what can I recast myself, when life without you is useless?*

You will forgive me for this madness. These words can only be written at night. The light of day is ruthless. It would not allow such words to be born. I am trying to leave behind this rhythm that is now inside of me—but it's impossible. Because you are the most important essence without which I cannot live on earth. Help me—write from time to time about love, simple as the grass, as the sun and the stars, as bread on a table, as the smile of a child. I only have to glimpse you—just for an instant—and it is for eternity.

I stopped reading, feeling suddenly like a spy, sneaking a peak through a keyhole on the private emotions of my parents. *This* was not the mother I knew.

I could not read the letters, not yet. I packed them into one of two large fire safes that I keep in the back of my closet. The safes contain a record of my life—about twenty-five diaries of varying shapes and sizes that I have filled compulsively since the age of eight. In the event that the house burns down, my life will be preserved.

I waited three months, until the strange lush trees of Virginia exploded in bloom, and I took the letters out again and began to read.

✿

Leningrad, U.S.S.R.
November 4, 1973

They met on a cold, wet day, the temperature holding at an even freezing. A slushy mixture of snow and rain fell from the leaden gray sky; the streets looked like slicked black ribbons and the leafless trees like monochrome sticks in the dim light of a northern autumn.

Irina dressed early for the party. She wore a long dress that she had knitted herself, beige with white stripes. She slipped her feet, which she considered much too large and wide, into black shoes with square toes. The three-inch heels made her stand nearly six feet tall. As she dressed she may have thought about the books she had read in the library that day, or about her feeling that her dissertation was burning her life away. Every day she took a bus to the library where she spent ten hours, reading an average of six books, many in French. She considered sleep a waste of time and slept only four hours a night. It made her angry that she had to sleep at all; she had so much to do. Maybe as she stood combing her hair, she thought about the writer Romain Rolland, the man of her work and of her dreams, the only man who understood her, though he was a Frenchman and had died of tuberculosis the year before she was born.

Paul did not go to the national archives because it was Sunday. Six days a week he made the hour-long walk from the island across Dvortsovii Bridge to the mainland, where Peter the Great in the guise of the Bronze Horseman marked his destination and greeted him; the czar, frozen in a posture of conquest atop his rearing stallion, kept watch over his capital. In the archives, Paul pored over ornately lettered manuscripts of the Petrine era and wrote notes on index cards, which he later filed into cardboard boxes decorated in paper made to look like green marble. Every evening he walked back in the chilly dusk, stopping for a cup of black coffee at the confectioner's. He walked everywhere he went, because he disliked the stuffiness and close contact of public transportation.

(In several weeks he would learn that he was known on the island as the crazy American, because he wore only thin trousers and a flannel shirt on his long treks across the city, while the Russians bundled themselves in scarves, raincoats, hats, and gloves.)

In the afternoon Paul walked to the cafeteria, a block away, where he ordered his favorite soup, *solyanka*, made of pickles, potatoes, meat, tomatoes, and sausages, served with a slab of crusty black bread. The soup tasted salty and sour from the pickles, and big blotches of orange-tinted fat floated on its claret surface. Paul found it filling and satisfying on a cold day, and the matronly woman who governed the colossal steel soup pot always ladled him a double serving. She wore a kerchief on her head and a wide apron stretched across her vast chest and stomach. Her cheeks glowed red in the steamy heat of the kitchen.

(Months later, Irina would learn that the woman, a Ukrainian, lavished the extra attention on Paul because she believed him to be a boy from her beloved Ukraine; she would be dismayed to learn that he was an American.)

They lived in a white five-story dormitory on Shevchenko, a quiet side street, on Vasilievsky Island, which lies in the crook formed where the Neva River splinters into two. Peter had built his city in a wet northern wilderness; from above the land appears crazed with waterways, like cracked glass. Three hundred graduate students lived in their dorm. Each room housed one or two foreigners and a Russian. Irina lived on the second floor in room 17, with a Canadian, Sarah, and Colette, who was French. Paul lived on the third floor in room 37, with a Russian, Petya. For three months they lived one floor apart and didn't meet.

Their windows both faced north, and they looked out over the same view, but his room, one floor up, and not directly over hers, offered a slightly different scene: a field with two or three poplar trees, patches of dying grass, and the roof of the movie theater Baltika just visible on the horizon. (Later, after Paul left, the field would be turned into a muddy construction site and would remain that way for the rest of Irina's stay.) Perhaps Paul stood looking out of the window that afternoon, thinking about the endless days of early August, when dusk didn't begin until after ten and it was dawn by four. Then, in September, the darkness of night began to stretch longer and longer; he now saw that the days of summer and winter were like photographic negatives of one another, dark replacing light, light replacing dark. It had snowed for the first time on September 26, and through all of October white flurries swirled in the sky, but they melted on contact with the ground; the streets, long and straight, meeting at right angles or in the knots of traffic circles, and perpetually wet, glistened like a black fisherman's net ensnaring the city. He thought of the lush evergreen citrus groves of his California hometown, and of cash registers; hardly a sliver of green could now be found in this grand, spacious city where glum store clerks impatiently cracked out sums on the hard blond and black beads of an abacus. He felt very alone, and the remaining seven months of his ten-month stay stretched out before him, a series of drab, wet, gray days and long walks back and forth over the bridge.

※

Riverside, California
1979

I watch my mother standing at the edge of a dusty field on a scorching day, pouring water out of a bowl into the dry earth basin around a spindly tree. She has no hose, no watering can, no proper tools for the job, and though I am only four, I can see that she will fail. Whatever it is she is trying to do by growing a birch tree here, she will fail. But I also understand that my mother will be happy only if the tree lives—this tree with its ghostly-white trunk, unlike any other tree that grows here. It's a ghost tree because it's from Russia and doesn't belong here. And my mother is a ghost mother because she doesn't belong here. She will never be the mother she would have been in Russia, but only a pale, thwarted version of her. My father has bought this birch tree for my mother because she told him that she misses the birches of Russia. But this scraggly, dying specimen cannot be what she means. I turn away from her and run into the other trees—mulberry, pepper, floss-silk, eucalyptus, jacaranda, peach, apricot, navel orange— the trees that thrive here, the trees that I am beginning to associate with home. I leave my mother standing with her dying tree, and I don't even look back.

❦

Riverside, California
May 1, 1983

Our mother lines up the three of us in the center of our cramped living room. We look at her expectantly. She is holding four identical objects that appear to be short lengths of wood with red cloth wound around them. She gives one of them a quick, dexterous snap, and the cloth is unfurled. I immediately recognize what it is—a miniature flag, the size of a post-card—and my breath hitches in my throat as I see the pale hieroglyph in the corner of a sea of continuous bright red. In Russian the word for red, *krasnii*, has the same root as the word for beautiful, *krasivii*.

I reach out and grasp the flag my mother is holding; its thin wooden handle, the size of a pencil, fits perfectly in my eight-year-old hand. Next my mother offers a flag to my sister, Natasha, and then to my brother, Sasha, who are nearing four and three. They awkwardly take hold of the smooth handles in their chubby hands and gaze at the bright scraps of color, their eyes round with wonder.

"We are having a parade," my mother announces in Russian.

"Why?" I answer in English, forgetting the rule.

"I can't understand you," my mother says firmly, fixing her eyes on some faraway point above my head.

I repeat the question in Russian: "*Pochemu?*"

"Because it is May Day; there are always parades on May Day," my mother replies.

I have seen the glossy Soviet magazines—*Ogonyok, Russkaya Zhizn*— full of color photographs of parades. The Soviets are always having parades; they march proudly through their wide city streets, carrying enormous portraits of Lenin and flying red banners with Soviet slogans on them. In the Soviet Union every day is a holiday, and it is always the first day of school. Schoolgirls in brown wool dresses and ruffled, starched white aprons are always leaving flowers at the eternal flame in remembrance of those who died for the Soviet cause. Every day there is a solemn, glorious occasion, but I miss it all, living on this deathly quiet suburban street where only an occasional falling palm frond cracking against the asphalt cuts through the stillness.

Natasha and Sasha, who do not yet recognize the flag, bring the red fabric up to their round faces and sniff. They have already learned that stuff from *there* has a particular smell—undeniably sweet and faintly musty, like a dry basement, like an old orange. I sniff my flag too; it has the scent. We know that scent from the books piled high in our living room, cliffs of precariously balanced books everywhere—the books my mother lugged with her when she came to America. These are our legacy—Pushkin, Tolstoy, Dostoevsky, Gogol, Chekhov, Lermontov, Turgenev, complete and unabridged in the original language. These are what my mother filled her suitcases with, not clothes or family photos. These are what would save her children from being swallowed by America.

"We will have our parade in the backyard," my mother says. "We certainly can't let ourselves be seen in the front yard."

"Why?" I ask, this time in Russian.

"Because we will be arrested."

"Why?" I gasp.

"Because this is America," she replies, leaving me to puzzle out the rest.

My green parakeet, named Ptichka, "birdie" in Russian, chirps angrily in his cage on the bookcase, and Natasha and Sasha begin to whop each other on the head with their flags. My mother unfurls the final flag—her own—and curls her broad hand around the handle. It looks like a toothpick with a scrap of red paper on it—the kind of thing stuck through sandwiches at delis—in her masculine hand, marbled with blue veins.

"Let's go," she says, leading the way through the sliding glass door onto our patio. We fall in line behind her single file, largest to smallest, like a family of ducklings waddling uncertainly behind the poised, somewhat oblivious mother duck.

My mother takes long, regular strides around our small backyard, passing by our strawberry patch, the steep hillside of ivy, the lemon tree, the turtle-shaped sandbox, the jungly rubber tree, the wire clothesline, and last we pass by the fence running along the neighbors' property, where my mother picks up her pace. The neighbors are black and breed rabbits in their yard. Their daughter, Wynette, who is a grade behind me in school, is my friend. My mother calls her Vinetka. She russifies all American names.

If your name is Andrew she will call you Andrei, if it is Kate she will call you Katya.

After two laps around the yard, Natasha and Sasha begin to fall behind. Sasha, bringing up the rear, drops on all fours near the rubber tree and starts picking in the dirt for bugs. Natasha keeps up for another lap, then stops at the strawberry patch, where she begins to poke around in the plants for berries. Our father has covered the strawberry patch in coffee grounds, because he read somewhere that coffee grounds make an excellent fertilizer. Our strawberry plants are massive and healthy, like the glossy-green plants of the fecund jungle, but the berries they produce are small, the size of peas. The coffee has stunted their growth. It has not stunted our father's growth; he is over six feet tall. He comes home each night smelling of acrid, pasty orange rind or saccharine orange blossoms, depending on the season; he loudly slurps soup at dinner, talks quietly to our mother in Russian, and occasionally swears at us in English when we're too boisterous.

My mother promenades on, her head high and aloof, and I hustle to keep up. She walks in great, even strides, her eyes focused on some grand thing far ahead of her; like a horse wearing blinders, she has no peripheral vision. I think she may be deaf as well. She is probably hearing the Soviet anthem blaring in her head; she is imagining herself parading among the happy Soviets. She does not seem to notice that she has lost two of her children. I do not fall behind. I am the only one of her children born in Russia, although the other two are considered Soviet citizens under Soviet law, because, according to our mother, it is a commonly known fact that nationality always passes through the mother.

I am still following my mother on the seventh and eighth laps, and I am almost out of breath. We are not parading, we are marching, and I am worried. Why is this dangerous? Why are we Soviet? What if Wynette sees me and tells the kids at school? This is my biggest worry. The kids at school call me a commie. I have told my mother this, who calmly replied, no, we are not communists, we are Soviet citizens. Such distinctions are lost on me. The kids have also informed me that as a commie I do not believe in God. I asked my mother: "What is God and why don't we believe in it?" "God is something that ignorant people believe in because they are afraid of the truth," she told me.

My mother is also worried, and maybe that is why she is striding so hard. She is worried that her children will be brainwashed. She has heard ugly, unthinkable propaganda in America; she has heard, for example, the vicious lie that Stalin murdered millions of people. She is afraid her children will grow up believing such things. When she learned that each morning at school I say the Pledge of Allegiance she was incensed. Her children are Soviet; they do not pledge allegiance to a foreign flag. She told me I did not have to say it, that I should refuse, but I never have the nerve.

My mother holds the dwarfed Soviet flag high above her head and marches onward. She never wanted to come to the United States. She was not an ardent communist, but neither was she a dissident. The man she fell in love with just happened to be an American graduate student— what could she do? She married my father with the understanding that he would return to the Soviet Union, and they would live there, but in four years of paper chases, he still had not been granted permission to go back. And by marrying an American my mother had committed professional suicide; she was not allowed to defend her dissertation, she suffered blow after blow in her career, and so she left. She went over to the other side, but in body only. Her finished but undefended dissertation sits in a trunk in our garage. If she had earned her PhD, we would be happy. If we lived where it snows in the winter instead of in the land of perpetual summer, we would be happy. If we were surrounded by white birches instead of mop-headed palms, we would be happy. Trees can make you happy, but we have the wrong kind. Snow can make you happy, but we have none. A language can make you happy, but this country speaks an alien one.

My mother finally stops near the rubber tree and pauses, for a moment keeping her austere head perfectly poised, and then she moves her gray eyes to survey the yard, blinking rapidly, as though she has just emerged from a dark cave into the sunny California afternoon. First she spots Sasha, who is still herding roly-polies; she briskly strides over to him and heaves him up under one arm, collecting his dusty flag in her other hand. Natasha is over in the corner of the yard, destroying leaves on the aloe vera plant in order to smear the sticky mucus over her bare legs. My mother, still carrying her wriggling son under one arm, slaps the aloe vera bits out of Natasha's hands and heaves her up under the other arm. One of my siblings begins to howl and struggle, and the other follows suit, while my mother carries them, like two sacks of flour, each slung carelessly under a muscled arm, into the house. She sets them down in the living room, side by side, where they continue to howl, and returns outside. I am still standing under the rubber tree where our parade ended. Without speaking, she plucks the flag out of my hand, then goes to retrieve the last flag, which Natasha has discarded under the lemon tree.

On her way back to the house my mother abruptly veers off course and walks to the fence that separates our property from the neighbors'. She peers suspiciously over the fence, her eyes narrowed, but seeing only the dopey rabbits nibbling on dandelions, she is satisfied and strides back to the house. I am left alone in the yard, with a nervy, fluttery feeling in my chest; we are surrounded by the enemy.

❧

Kuybyshev, U.S.S.R.
High summer, 1984

We are at the dacha, prowling in the lush tangled growth of summer fruit. Within reach are raspberries, gooseberries, currants, strawberries, plums, cherries, and apples. I am nine, and I am gorging myself on sweetness. Trailing me are Natasha, five, and Sasha, four. This is the first time my mother and I have been back since we left in 1978. Natasha and Sasha have never been here before. My father has stayed in America to work.

I hold a gooseberry up to the sky: a perfect miniature watermelon. We don't have these in California. We don't have currants either, or white plums. Our grandmother, Babushka, comes marching by, hauling a metal pail full of potatoes. She spent the morning worrying over the strawberry patch. She now chastises Natasha for wiping her juice-stained fingers on her clothes. She chastises Sasha for cramming his mouth too full. She chastises me, the eldest, for not watching over my sister and brother. Then she sighs deeply, resigned to her fate, and sets off on another chore. Our grandparents speak only Russian, and deep into our Russian summer, we, too, now speak only Russian.

I have learned that Babushka operates in two modes: she is either chastising, or she is lamenting. "Oh, my heart hurts!" she cries out, several times a day. "My heart hurts at the thought that you will be leaving. First I counted in months the time that you had left, and now in weeks, and soon it will be days, and then hours! I can't bear it!" I don't understand these sudden outbursts of emotion. My parents are cool, undemonstrative. But Babushka is like a pipe so full of pressure that she must periodically burst open, the emotions gushing. *"Moi rodniye,"* she calls us, again and again. She tells me that the Soviet Union is my *rodina*. It is a word without a precise English translation. Perhaps *native* is the closest: my native people, my native land. But these people, this land do not feel *rod-niye* to me. My grandparents and my aunt Olga are not my native people. Most of the time, I am choked with homesickness. I want my American house, my American grandparents. I want orange groves and palm trees. The dacha is the only place where the homesickness dislodges from my throat. We spend most of our days cooped up in my grandparents' down-town apartment, four adults, three children, and a cat congesting the two rooms. The space is choked with cots and toys and laundry hanging to dry.

Natasha is tugging on my arm. "Dr Pepper," she pleads. "I want Dr Pepper."

"There is no Dr Pepper here," I inform her.

"Dr Pepper!" she shouts, suddenly on the verge of a tantrum. She is tired; there is much that she has had to get used to. Our brother, crouched down in the strawberry patch, watches us.

"There is no Dr Pepper," I say firmly. "This is Russia."

"I want to drink Dr Pepper!" she wails.

Our grandfather, Dyedushka, who has been picking apples nearby, approaches. "What is it she wants to drink?" he asks me.

"Dr Pepper," I reply.

"Dok-tor Peh-prrr," he echoes. "Aha, dok-tor peh-prrr." He sets off deci-sively in the direction of the house, as though he knows precisely what he is going after. Like Babushka, he is a mystery to me. A taciturn man, he occa-sionally throws out a wry comment, then falls back into silence. Short and solid, he is of peasant stock, a descendant of serfs. I know several pertinent facts about him: he was one of five children, but he left his village, went to school, became an engineer. He has the same name as my brother: Sasha, Aleksandr, Alexander. He was born before the Revolution of 1917. And most intriguing of all: he doesn't know when his birthday is. His mother, working in a field, simply paused from her chores long enough to have a baby, then went back to work. It was the middle of summer, she told him, and so he celebrates his birthday on July 15. This makes him mythic in my eyes, a sur-vivor from another age.

Dyedushka returns, holding a glass full of a ruby liquid, which he is stirring with a spoon. He offers the glass to my sister.

"Dok-tor Peh-prrr," he announces.

Natasha takes the glass and sniffs the beverage with suspicion. She hes-itantly takes a sip. "Mmmm," she says, then begins to chug the drink.

"Dr Pepper," Sasha whines from the strawberries.

"Alright, come with me," Dyeduskha says.

We all follow him back to the house, which isn't a house at all but a train caboose that was planted here among the raspberry bushes many decades ago. It's been partitioned into two rooms, a lumpy bed in each. Besides these, there are just a scarred wooden table, several stools, a couple of naked light bulbs dangling from the ceiling, and a single-burner electric stove. We stand around Dyedushka at the table as he begins to make more of the mysterious beverage.

Our mother is in the shadowy corner of the room, sitting on the bed with her back against the wall, a book propped in her lap. She hardly glances up. She is not interested in the outdoors. She is not interested in cooking or cleaning. She always performs these chores angrily, defiantly. Our mother reads and writes and thinks. She is an intellectual. She is usually doing two or three things at one time: reading while watching TV, knitting while listening to music, writing while supervising her children. She hardly sleeps at all.

My mother has become more of a mystery to me. I had believed that upon returning to the Soviet Union—*home*—she would finally be happy. Much of the time, she does have a new levity, especially when she makes the rounds, visiting all her old friends, but there are melancholy moods as well, when she retreats from the world: when she reads, when she writes letters to our father. She does not talk to her parents a great deal.

This is my grandfather's recipe for Dr Pepper: crushed raspberries, currants, gooseberries, cherries, and strawberries with a generous spoonful of sugar topped off with fresh well water and briskly stirred. We drink one glass, two, and demand more. It is the best Dr Pepper we have ever tasted. Natasha never mentions that Dyedushka's Dr Pepper bears little resemblance to the carbonated saccharine beverage that we have back home. Perhaps she has forgotten how Dr Pepper tastes. Perhaps the words are just an echo from home, a reaching out for the language she is losing. Perhaps, in asking for something for which she has no name, she seizes the first words that floated to the surface of her mind: Dr Pepper. Perhaps she means: *home, affection, attention, love.* Perhaps, like me, she means: *I am homesick. I do not understand this place. Please give me something familiar that I can hold and taste.*

Riverside, California
1987

I don't know the date of that particular argument. I don't even know what the argument was about. I was twelve, and my mother and I argued frequently. I noted many—but not all—of the arguments in my diary. On January 26, I wrote: "She said she never wanted to see me again, and she meant it. I hate her, and I mean it." On February 9, I wrote: "She says that I don't exist. She never talks to me, never pays any attention to me. . . . I'm a failure in my mother's eyes. I'm not learning Russian, I don't talk Russian at home. If she could she'd send me to an orphanage." On May 14, I wrote what she said to me that day: "You'll probably drop out of school after ninth grade, get married, and have thirteen kids."

I am surly and disrespectful; I suspect my parents are idiots, and I tell them so. I believe I know so much more about everything than they do. I declare my hatred for classical music and everything Russian, especially the language. I speak only English—a slangy, mumbling English—and I don't read books in any language. Night after night, my mother and I yell at each other, my father standing by nervously, helpless. If I were asked the reasons for my anger, I would be utterly inarticulate. My rage is beyond the reach of language.

Arguments inevitably end with me crying in my room. I don't even consider what my mother might be doing or feeling. I pound my pillow and mash my face into it. I listen for my mother, but she never comes. I wish that I had the sort of mother who would come back when we were both calm; we would apologize and embrace. I do not have that sort of mother.

That night, we are arguing—again. I am sitting on my bed, shouting something nasty to my mother. Perhaps I am saying that she is stupid and I hate her. Perhaps I call her a bitch. I know that word in Russian, and I use it more than once. It's about the only word I say to her in Russian anymore. Whatever I say, my mother's anger suddenly reaches a new pitch.

"I almost got an abortion when I was pregnant with you!" she screams at me. "I wish I did!"

She is so enraged she is in tears. She could kill me, I think. She leaves the room, and for the first time, I do not wish her to return. This time, I take the awful thing she has tossed at me and gulp it down, keeping it inside like a terrible secret. It is something barbed and sweet at the same time. It is like a weapon that is graceful but deadly. She will be sorry, I vow. Perhaps she thinks I should be grateful merely for being given life. But I demand so much more. And I will show her.

❦

Riverside, California
June 1, 1990

Before I picked up a chair from the patio and threw it through the sliding door, shattering the glass in a blast of shards;

before I stepped through the jagged hole into the living room to defiantly face my gawking parents;

before I said smugly, "You didn't think I'd do it, huh?";

before my mother ran to the phone to call the police,

these are the things that happened that day:

I had three nightmares: in the first, I was being eaten alive by piranhas; in the second, I was being tickled to death aboard a Greyhound bus; in the third, I witnessed a deadly, fiery bus crash. I refused to go to school. I spent most of the day sitting in my room, smoking and writing in my diary. I wrote a poem. My mother took away my last pair of shoes to prevent me from leaving the house. When I did leave the house, I put on a pair of her shoes. I met up with some friends, and we split a bottle of Strawberry Hill. I returned home at eleven o'clock that night to find myself locked out. A note on the door indicated that I was to sleep outside. Three blankets and a pillow had been left on a table in the backyard. I rang the doorbell. I knocked on the sliding glass door. I knew my parents were just inside, watching television.

"I suggest you open the door. It's against the law to leave me out here!" I yelled through the door.

"No, at Tough Love they said we could do this," my father called back. We shouted in English.

"I suggest you open the door."

"No, I'm not going to let you get your way."

"If you don't let me in, I'm going to break this door down. You don't think I will?" I pounded on the glass with my fists.

"No, I don't think you're that crazy."

So I showed him that I was.

Before the police officer came and told my parents that they could not lock their fifteen-year-old out of the house at night;

before he came to my room in order to find out whether I was sober;

before my mother came tearing through the house in a rage, screaming at me while I sat placidly writing in my diary about the day's events,

these are the things that happened the previous month:

I ran away from home to Mississippi on a Greyhound bus. My father came out to the Picayune, Mississippi, jail to take me home. My parents took my door off its hinges and disconnected my cable TV. They nailed my windows shut. I rarely went to school. I was flunking out of the ninth grade. I smashed dishes on the kitchen floor while screaming at my parents. I drank and did drugs. I sliced gashes into both arms from my wrist to the bend of my elbow with a razor blade. I was evaluated by psychiatrists.

Before my mother screamed at me (in Russian) that she wished she had aborted me;

before I calmly retorted (in English) that she might as well not waste her breath because I didn't give a fuck;

before my mother ran crying into the living room;

before I heard her say to my father that she was going to commit suicide if I lived under the same roof with her;

before I reveled in her cruelty and pain, thinking, *You see, she is horrible to me, you see the horror I must live with, you see how my life is all busted to hell because of her, you see why I will never, never, never be like her,*

this is what happened:

I learned to write the words *I LOVE YOU* in English when I was five years old. I painstakingly wrote these words on a piece of paper and delivered the message to my mother. She was washing dishes. She read the note and handed it back to me. "It's not in Russian," she told me, turning back to the sink. I did not know how to write the words in Russian. I went to my father for help. I handed him a sheet of paper and a pen. I commanded him to write the words in Russian. I took the new message to my mother. She glanced at my father's familiar cursive, and responded, "You didn't write that yourself." I did not go back a third time.

After writing many, many words in my diary that summer;

after writing, "The only way I can possibly stay sober is if I do it for myself," and, "There is only one stable thing in my empty life now, and that's my writing";

after my first poem appeared in print, and my mother said, "You're finally becoming a person," and I asked, "Wasn't I a person before?" and my mother said, "No, you were just a girl, but to be published makes you a person";

after two months passed,

my mother and I—just the two of us—would go back to Russia,

and this is what would happen:

Boarding the plane, I would say to her, "You'd better bring me back. You'd better not leave me in Russia." And once there, I would say, "I don't want to go back. Leave me here." But she wouldn't. In my grandparents' apartment, I would listen to Nautilus Pompilius on my aunt's old phonograph, singing along in Russian the words of despair: *I broke glass like chocolate in my hand.* I would drum out stories and poems on an antediluvian manual typewriter. I would carry a small notebook with me everywhere and write down all that I saw and heard. I would walk in a forest with my grandfather for the last time, at his pace, slowly, and he would tell me the names of the strange trees, and he would stoop low beneath the canopies, searching for the edible mushrooms that would be our dinner together. Before we boarded the train to go back to Moscow, my grandparents, elderly and stooped, would kiss me good-bye, and I would think, *These are my mother's parents.* And I would think, *This is the last time I will see them. I will never see them again.* And I did not.

❧

Leningrad, U.S.S.R.

November 4, 1973

Life in room 17 orbited a sturdy, round wooden table: six feet in diameter, draped in a burgundy tablecloth and covered in cup rings, crumbs, books, pens, a stray soup pot, sugar granules, teaspoons, cards from a scattered deck. Every night half a dozen to a dozen students of different nationalities—Russian, English, French, German, American, Finnish—gathered at the table to drink tea and talk from ten until two or three in the morning. Irina always said that you could seat any number of people at a round table, and it proved true, night after night. On her twenty-eighth birthday in October, fifteen French students gathered in the room for the celebration. When the five or six mismatched chairs filled, people piled onto the beds. A haze of cigarette smoke cloaked the room, curling in a delicate white filigree, collecting in a dense blanket on the ceiling. Irina did not smoke and often opened the small hinged window to diffuse the thick clouds.

Room 37, the same size as 17, had two beds instead of three. Paul's bed stood to the left of the window. Paul and Petya studied quietly at the square table in the center of the room. Petya was studying political economy. Occasionally he asked Paul how much something cost in America. Otherwise, he tended to be quiet. Coming from the warm, southern republic of Kazakhstan, he sometimes complained of the cold and kept a thermometer in the room that he monitored regularly. Paul, despite his California roots, seemed impervious to the cold.

(Later, when the temperature in room 37 would fall to eleven degrees Celsius, Petya would buy a space heater to supplement the feeble heat put out by the radiator under the window.)

Irina and her friend Galya served as the cultural directors in the dormitory. Galya, from Tomsk, had ivory hair that she wore in a thick twisted rope falling down her back nearly to her knees. She and her husband, Valera, lived across the hall and a few doors down from room 17. As cultural directors, Irina and Galya organized the series of evening parties hosted in turn by every nation represented in the dorm. The inaugural party, the Russian samovar, always fell on the Sunday closest to November 7, the day of the October Revolution.

(In February, the French would decide to celebrate their cultural evening by preparing French onion soup, and Irina would lead them around Leningrad, collecting six enormous soup pots from the cafeteria, one hundred bottles of white wine, sixty pounds of cheese, and two mountains of onions.)

Irina and Galya walked down the stairs together to the spacious room on the first floor. The study tables, pushed together to form one large U-shaped table, were draped in satin tablecloths, the bright red of the flag. Irina and Galya arranged trays and plates of pastries, *pryaniki*, and candy, and they placed cups and teapots at regular intervals along the table. The teapots, gathered from all the rooms, formed a motley collection. The two teapots from room 17 had made their way down here: a green enamel one and a porcelain one decorated in a spray of blossoms on a milky background. A record player piped out Russian folk ballads and Revolutionary songs in the corner. Irina set out the last teapots with great haste, maybe splattering the tablecloths with hot water droplets, clinking the porcelain cups together; her manner, brusque and impatient, suggested that there wasn't enough time in her one life to get everything done. She was forever racing time: especially since the doctors had taken an entire year from her. Five months previous they released her from the sanatorium with good news: she was cured of tuberculosis. But she had lost so much time, and she did not know if the cure would last.

While Irina and Galya were making a final check of the tables, in room 37 Petya broke the long evening silence by announcing: "It's time to drink tea." Paul put on the only suit he'd ever owned (bought for his high school graduation thirteen years before) and followed Petya down the two flights of stairs. They found two seats together. Paul poured his tea: first splashing bitter black *zavarka* in the bottom of his cup, then filling it to the brim with hot water.

About 120 people were at the party. Paul and Petya, two of the quietest people there, sat side by side drinking tea and not speaking. Maybe Paul looked at the bank of wide windows along the wall and studied the reflection of yellow light and red tablecloth, the shimmering opaque blackness of the world beyond. Maybe he sampled a *pryanik* and found it too hard and sweet. Maybe he picked up a piece of candy and studied the ornate label, reading the name of the factory and city in Russian: *Fabrika Rossiya, Kuybyshev.*

❧

Riverside, California
September, 1998
My mother and I are sitting at the table in my parents' house, studying Russian. We are struggling with cases. Russian has six; English has none. I have trouble memorizing rules and exceptions to rules. I can often hear whether something is correct in Russian without having the slightest idea why. My mother calls my knowledge "instinctive," but instinct will get me only so far. I need to know the rules and how to apply them.

I have gone back to school to finish my BA; I am majoring in comparative literature with an emphasis in Russian literature. (I flunked out of the last university I attended, but my mother doesn't know this. She thinks I merely dropped out to work full time.) I have not lived at home for over three years. I come two or three times a week for my lessons. My mother and I are polite to one another. My sister and brother still live at home, but they have their own lives. My brother, the youngest, has just graduated from high school. Neither of them speaks Russian anymore.

My mother is patient. I make mistakes; she explains things more than once. We review the cases again: nominative, genitive, dative, accusative, instrumental, prepositional. I do not like to think of language in these terms. I want it to be natural and beautiful.

Halfway through the lesson, my mother makes a comment: "Your father is the only person I've ever known who has a natural gift for languages."

I know this is true. Languages have never come easy to me. I failed French in high school. But I also know that she is making the comment about herself as well as me. Her English will never be as good as mine; my Russian will never be as good as hers. We do the best we can. We try. My mother teaches at a university now; she lectures in English. I am studying Russian, however belatedly. I am not bad, but I am not eloquent. My Russian professor at the university has a computer program that has determined my pronunciation of Russian sounds "fluent." I feel far from it, though my pronunciation is better than anyone else's in the class, including the professor's. Russian is the only language I knew until I was three and a half. It is my native tongue, but it is foreign. English is my fluent language, but it is not my first. I wrestle with them both, trying to bridge the gap that can never be closed.

We turn back to the lesson. The declension of numbers is nearly unendurable to me. We try again.

❧

St. Petersburg, Russia
July, 1999

I have returned to Russia for the first time in nine years, for the first time since the fall of the Soviet Union, and for the first time alone. I am in St. Petersburg with a group of Americans. They are here to talk about reading and writing, to see the sights. Ostensibly, I am here for those reasons, too. But I have a hidden motive. I walk the streets for hours—looking for something, I can't say what. I don't sleep. The days and nights bleed together in a perpetually gray-white sky. I scrutinize the city for signs at all times. I watch the bridges on the Neva raise their arms to let the ships pass, night after night, because others have done this before me and have found meaning in it.

Thanks to my mother, my Russian is still with me. As long as I don't have to make sustained conversation, people don't even notice an accent. I can get around undetected, an imposter, pretending to be a Russian. I walk up and down Nevsky Prospekt. I gawk at the Hermitage. I wander into neighborhoods far from the showcase streets, where ramshackle apartment buildings lean, bricks crumble, the city sags. And then I go back over to the other side. I sit on the steps of the Kazanskii Cathedral, drinking beer with my fellow Americans. We go to Internet cafes to check our e-mail.

Pushkin is everywhere. It is the bicentenary of the poet's birth. He looks down at me from banners, from posters; I buy a commemorative matchbook with his image. His words gallop through my mind, thanks to my mother. I glimpse the ghost of Gogol's Akakii Akakievich slinking down a side street, thanks to my mother. I see Dostoevsky's lovers drifting through the white nights. I see the steadfast figure of Anna Akhmatova standing outside the prison walls, all thanks to my mother. My mind brims over with the literature of this place. My mother read it all to me, in the melodic and sharp-edged Russian language, night after night, throughout my childhood. These were my bedtime stories.

I think about this city first rising out of a foggy no man's land, erected upon one man's vision and the bones of the men who died here. Toiling in this far end of the earth, they translated their human flesh into city. On the banks of the Neva, in the opal bloom of a white night, I can almost make out the ghostlike figure of Peter the Great, standing, gesturing, commanding—that bigger-than-life czar who looked to the West to bring Russia out of darkness. Here I stand, in most European Russia, in most Western Russia: this city, a melding of Russia and the West; this city, a translation of Europe into Russian; this city, a child of both, inheriting all the best characteristics from both parents.

I stand looking up at Falconet's statue of Peter the Great. I think of the translation of one man's vision into city, the translation of czar into bronze. I think of Pushkin's "The Bronze Horseman," a translation of statue into poem, resurrecting the man, the czar, the vision. All art is translation.

I think of all that has happened in this place: the revolutions, the siege, the corpses in the streets. I think of how this city has been made and remade, names given, names revoked: St. Petersburg, Petrograd, Leningrad. My mind cannot hold it all.

I am looking at Peter the Great atop his horse. I always knew I would return here, to this place I had never been, my mother fleeing it, flying home to Kuybyshev in a snowstorm a month before my birth. I was almost here before. I am what my parents conceived in Leningrad, the product of their love, its independent agent, going forth into the world. But I am not in Leningrad. I was conceived in a place that no longer exists and born in a place that no longer exists. Like St. Petersburg, Kuybyshev, my birth city, has remade itself, taking on its former name: Samara. I have never been to Samara. In a week, I will be traveling there, to see my remaining relatives: my mother's sister, and a five-year-old cousin whom I've never met.

I am looking at the Bronze Horseman, but he hardly seems there at all. It is as though I am seeing the statue in a dream. It is as though I am looking at a picture in a book—and that other one, the one in my memory, is the real one. I cannot wipe from my eyes the cobwebs of the years, the long life of not being here—not being here so acutely, so passionately, so intensely, that the actual being here is dulled to a dream. I have seen this all before, in a book, in a film, in the words of my parents. I have seen it all, and I have lived it more intensely. I have no vision left for the real thing. The myth of this city—this city that I sprung from but had never been to—is so vivid that I cannot see past it. I am in a state of torpor, viewing the shimmering surfaces of beautiful things, but they are only toy castles, toy monuments, a toy city on a toy river.

I search and search the city for something I cannot find.

※

Herndon, Virginia
July 3, 2004

Outside, heat curls up off the sidewalks and the streets, the humidity thick and muffling. Inside, the air conditioner thrums, pumping cool air through our house. I have been transcribing and translating the letters all day. I am typing them, rendering them in English. This is a beginning. I am far from writing my book. There remains much to be done. I am dissatisfied with my progress. I spend more time staring out the window at the white pines and sugar maple than I do working.

The word *translation*, it seems, does not belong only to me, a literary person, a person of words. It means many things to many people.

Translation: Transference; removal or conveyance from one person, place, or condition to another. Transference of a disease from one person or part of the body to another. The action or process of turning from one language into another; also, the product of this; a version in a different language. The expression or rendering of something in another medium or form (of a painting by an engraving or etching). Transformation, alteration, change; changing or adapting to another use; renovation. A transfer of property; alteration of a bequest by transferring the legacy to another person.

I have just learned today that a tiny new life is unfurling within me: the translation of my own and my husband's genetic code. I cannot yet say how I feel about this fact.

To translate: To carry or convey to heaven without death. To move (a body) from one point or place to another without rotation. To express in other words, to paraphrase. To use (genetic information in messenger RNA) to determine the amino-acid sequence of a protein during its synthesis. To interpret, explain; to expound the significance of; to express (one thing) in terms of another. To change in form, appearance, or substance; to transmute; to transform, alter; of a tailor, to renovate, turn, or cut down (a garment). To transport with the strength of some feeling; to enrapture, entrance.

And all of this is true. I am doing all of this, and more. It is no small feat. I read back through the letters on my computer. I am losing something in translation. Their meaning is in their bilingualism, their duality, their two voices, interweaving; their meaning is inextricable from this twining of languages, this twining of selves, one wrapping around the other, like the double helix of DNA. I am that infant cradled in my parents' words of 1975. Cradled within me, a new life blooms, translating forth into flesh another generation.

In these words scattered on a page are the things I have lost in translation, the things I have found in translation.

❧

Lincoln, Nebraska

January 1, 2007

The meteorologists predict only a dusting of snow, but we get nearly eight inches. On this first day of a new year, the world outside is blanketed in white. We look at the yard through the windows, then warm ourselves by the fire. My parents, who have been visiting since Christmas Eve, are scheduled to leave later today.

My daughter—Katherine, Kate, Katya—is busy cooking in her new play kitchen. She has appropriated all her other gifts—rubber toys for the tub, a stuffed blackbird, a basket of fluffy toy kittens—for use in her culinary efforts. She is currently cooking up a blue rubber crocodile in a frying pan. My parents, my husband, and I are sitting around the living room, watching her. My mother is also knitting, because she never does just one thing at a time.

I am in a PhD program. I am still writing my book. This year, I will turn thirty-two, my daughter will turn two, my mother will turn sixty-two.

"Crocodile ready!" Katherine cries, running over to my mother—her babushka—to offer her a taste.

"That's very good," my mother says, in English.

Kate takes the crocodile over to my father, her dyedushka, who is filming her with his camcorder.

"*Deba*," she says. "Try." She has not mastered the words *baba* and *dyeda*. She has conflated them into one word: *deba*. She seems to apply it indiscriminately to both grandparents.

Momentarily losing interest in cooking, Kate runs behind the sofa and crouches down, hiding. She waits.

"*Gde Katya?*" my mother calls. "*Gde Katya?*" Where is Katya?

"*Gde Katya?*" Kate echoes her, giggling. Then she runs out into the middle of the living room. "Here's Katya!" she cries.

"*Vot Katya!*" my mother exclaims. Here is Katya.

My father, camcorder in hand, goes to the window to peer nervously out at the snow again. The cold white stuff still seems a bit foreign to me as well, but I have lived four years in Virginia, almost three in Nebraska. I am getting used to it.

Kate is cooking once more, cramming a gray stuffed animal into her oven. She knows only a smattering of Russian words: *gusenitsa* (caterpillar), *krasnii* (red). My husband does not speak Russian, and I am sloppy, inconsistent, throwing out Russian phrases here and there, then forgetting for weeks to say even a word.

"Baked cat," Kate announces, offering me her creation.

"That is delicious," I tell my daughter. "That is the most delicious cat I have ever tasted." My tone is not as effusive as I intend it to be.

Before heading for the airport, we are going to see my brother, Alex, who lives two blocks away. It is time to get bundled up for the short walk.

My parents are growing old. My mother is calm now, kind. Her children are grown; she has a career. She did in fact become a professor—two decades later, in America. She is successful. She seems fond of us, her grown children. We can make her laugh. Maybe she misses us, now that we're not constantly underfoot, now that we don't stand in her way. I feel protective toward her. I want to apologize for something—I can't say what precisely—but we still leave the most important things unsaid. I can write it down. As always, I can write it all down.

We are dressed. I am holding Katya, bundled in a snowsuit. My father is already out on the porch, filming the street. My mother is adjusting her boots.

"Mama," I say. "It's time."

❊

West Hartford, Connecticut
Spring 2012

My four-year-old son is a plant watcher. He notices when flowers bloom, when the garlic sends up shoots, when the trees leaf out. He asks me to buy him potted plants when he sees them in stores. He grows petunias and impatiens. He's particularly interested in the progress of the multitrunked birch that we planted in the front yard when we moved here nearly two years ago. He watches it anxiously. He wants to know, *Will it fall over? Will it die? Will its leaves fall off?* For now, it's flourishing. *Is it time to water the birch?* Yes, I tell him. It's time. He fills his watering can and sets to work.

❊

Leningrad, U.S.S.R.
November 4, 1973

Irina noticed him first. She became aware that there was a very quiet man sitting beside her who had no one to talk to. She waited five minutes, and then out of politeness, she spoke to him. She asked him questions about his work: What was he studying? What was his dissertation on? And he told her, in correct but slightly accented Russian, that he was studying Stefan Yavorskii, the acting patriarch of the Russian Orthodox Church during the Petrine era. Yavorskii had gone to Jesuit College in Poland and knew Latin, Greek, Polish, Ukrainian, Church Slavonic, and Old Russian, but he wrote primarily in a combination of the Polish alphabet and the Church Slavonic language. Irina was impressed that he knew so much about Old Russian. They spoke politely to one another and used the formal form of you: *vi*.

At first, Irina thought that he looked Russian. After she heard him speak, she decided that his accent sounded Ukrainian. He certainly looked Ukrainian: bright blue eyes, round cheeks, dark brown hair, balding. She noticed that he wore a very outdated black suit with narrow trouser legs. She was surprised when she asked him where he was from and he told her America. Sometime during the conversation they told one another their first names: Irina, Paul.

He looked into the face of the woman talking to him—at her widely spaced, intelligent gray eyes, her long, straight nose, her broad face with a cleft in the chin, her strong, square jaw—and he saw that she was very beautiful. He felt bashful and inarticulate.

At the end of the conversation, she said to him: "If you ever want to have tea, come to room 17. Remember: room 17." And he remembered. But that night he was not among those at the round table, nor was he there the following night, and Irina thought that he would never come, because in her experience people came on the first or second night or not at all.

(Four days later, on November 8, he would knock on the door of room 17 for the first time. A week later, on November 11, the snow would accumulate, the city would turn a soft luminous white, and she would take him shopping for a winter hat made of black rabbit with flaps that came over the ears. Irina would cut the eight-foot-long blue scarf given her by an old student exactly in half; she would give half to Paul and keep half herself, and they would wear matching scarves all winter. They would walk together among the snowy pines near Tsarskoe Selo and take one another's picture with Paul's camera. On March 20, they would marry. On May 1, they would watch the May Day demonstrations and cross half the city on foot. At Peterhof Palace they would walk among the birch trees together. In the forest Irina would wash her hands in a cold stream and Paul would warm them for her. On June 5, he would return to America, alone.)

During that first meeting, they talked for no more than three minutes. He thought she was very beautiful. She thought he seemed very lonely. The party continued. Neither of them had any sense that something remarkable had happened. At nine or ten they all went back to their rooms. Outside the icy rain churned out of the sky and fell steadily in the darkness.

Quercus

There is some basic sympathy between oaks and humans. We both like the same things, we both have similar virtues, and we have both spread to the very limits of what we like. And wherever we have gone, oaks have become central to our daily lives. We invented a whole way of living out of their fruit and their wood, and by that token, they invented us too.

—WILLIAM BRYANT LOGAN,
OAK: THE FRAME OF CIVILIZATION

WHEN I WAS just out of high school and thought I wanted to be a journalist, I spent close to four years working at several local daily newspapers in California. I wrote about hockey players and real estate agents, about preachers and bowlers, about criminals and mountain men. And often, as I gathered information for a story, I would feel the tug of those other lives that I glimpsed. For a day or an hour, I would mentally abandon my own life and imagine myself as someone else. I wanted to be a convert to another life.

For an afternoon, I dedicated my life to teaching pottery to senior citizens. I became a pyrotechnician and wowed thousands with my stunning fireworks displays. I joined the Seventh-day Adventist Church to become a follower of the charismatic black woman pastor I interviewed. I married the young, God-fearing trucker I met at a truck-stop chapel; he was from Pennsylvania and looking for, among other things, a wife. I became a classic-car buff and renovated a 1952 midnight-blue Chevy Fleetline. I spent a day at a monastery and wanted to join up, to become a nun and devote my life to ritual—if only I believed in God. I became a Master Gardener and lost myself forever among the forsythia. I trained to be a computer programmer and learned to design GIS programs for police to use in mapping crimes on a nationwide grid. When the Texan high school football players—whom I had come to interview to find out how much they ate—asked me what I was doing later, I became the kind of party girl who hung out late with athletes. I went to medical school to learn how to perform heart transplants on nine-year-old boys, like the one I wrote about, the one whose photo I took as he clutched a Winnie the Pooh doll in his hospital bed.

Daily I sought conversion: something powerful and sudden like a tornado to seize me up and shake me senseless, something to ravish me, to take me in its clutches forever and never set me back on earth. But working at daily newspapers, every day the view was different, the religion changed, the weather turned, the story was new. I never studied anything at length, I never knew anything in depth. I ran from one story to the next, my knowledge rudimentary. I was promiscuous in my yearnings, my many aborted passions. I took cuttings from all those lives, lined them up on a windowsill, where they shriveled, and all that remains now are yellowing clips in three-ring binders.

Now I am a dozen years removed from that life. Now what I want to learn most is how to stay put, how to be a student not of the sensational and transient but of the commonplace, the everyday, the enduring. Now instead of leaves of newspaper print, I collect a different kind of leaves, the real deal. Now I have become the student of a tree.

OAK

This summer when we bought our house in Omaha, we became the owners of, among other things, a medium-sized, middle-aged pin oak in the front yard. To claim that we own a rooted creature over sixty feet tall has a strange ring to it. The tree does not admit to being owned, nor is it likely to know that it has changed hands. It requires only that those who control the land where it lives are generous—or negligent—enough to allow it life.

I sat in the tree's generous shade through the muggy days, and I waited to learn something, to be told some news.

IN BRIEF

Working at newspapers gave me the opportunity to live many lives vicariously. And, as it turned out, it also allowed me to suffer many deaths vicariously. A large part of my job was to report on crime. Twice daily—first thing in the morning and last thing in the evening—I would make a round of calls to the local police and fire stations, asking for the news. On my desk the police scanner chattered incessantly. I ignored the routine traffic stops, the chest pains, the shoplifters, the domestic disturbances, and listened for the things that mattered: injury accidents, structure fires, homicides.

When the news warranted a story, the editor would assign an inch count based on the perceived importance of the event. "Give me twelve inches on that fire," the editor would bark. Or, "I want fifteen inches on the homicide." Sometimes, as a story developed, its significance increased or diminished. It was important to get an ID on a homicide victim as soon as possible—to deem the importance of the death, and to seek out family members for comment. It wasn't a science, and editors often made judgment calls, but the general system was followed by everyone. At a newspaper, the perceived importance of anything—even a life—could be measured in inches.

Often, however, an event wasn't deemed worthy of a full story, and then the editor would say, "Make it a brief." Since I was a junior member of the staff, I spent more of my time writing briefs, the small news, rather than bylined stories, the big news. The more senior reporters got most of the high-profile crimes. I wrote two- and three- and four-paragraph briefs that ran in a daily column titled *Crime and Fire Reports*. I wrote hundreds of them; I have an entire three-ring binder devoted just to police briefs.

For example: I wrote about the body of a fifty-year-old homeless man that was discovered by garbage collectors when they emptied their truck at the landfill. He spilled out with the rest of the trash. His relatives said they hadn't heard from him in over a year and as far as they knew, he was homeless. The police suspected "he was already dead when trash collectors unknowingly picked up the body from a dumpster in a residential area."

OAK

The oak is the United States' National Tree. There are more than eighty species in the United States, and somewhere between five hundred and six hundred species in the world. It is America's most widespread hardwood and the most widely distributed of forest trees. It is ubiquitous and profoundly adaptable.

In *Oak: The Frame of Civilization*, William Bryant Logan writes, "It was the great virtue of oaks that they responded not by specializing and narrowing their range, but by adapting, expanding, and radiating into more and wider-flung landscapes. There have seldom been creatures as tenacious as oaks, but their staying power is founded on their own ability to change." He may well have been describing human beings. Oaks spread all over the world, and this one in my front yard landed in Omaha. I, too, have traveled far to settle here.

IN BRIEF

There was often a fine line between a brief and a story. What might be a brief on one day would have been a story on another. There were a number of factors that the editor weighed in making the determination: Was it a busy news day? How much room was in the paper? Did the crime occur in our core coverage area or on the margins? Did it occur where we had a large number of subscribers or just a few? How serious was the crime? How exceptional was the crime? How much could the police tell us? And finally, what was the life worth?

The dead man on the Greyhound bus was a brief. He was returning to Southern California from Las Vegas. "When the bus stopped, everybody got off but him," the investigator said. The seventy-five-year-old man apparently quietly died of a heart attack, and no one noticed. And now, reading over the brief, I wonder who that man was, traveling to and from Vegas alone on a Greyhound bus. I know nothing about him, and yet, what I do know makes me think he was profoundly lonely, that his fate was profoundly sad. The police claimed no crime was committed, but I am not so sure.

OAK

My daughter spends an afternoon collecting acorns in her bicycle helmet, and then she redistributes them, hiding most of them inside our house. In *The Tree*, Colin Tudge writes, "Animals cannot afford to run charities, and they must have their quid pro quo. Sometimes they expect to eat a proportion of the seeds, and so squirrels typically consume at least as many acorns as they scatter." I don't know what, if anything, the acorns do for my daughter. She is not getting nutrition from them. I think my daughter *is* running a charity.

For weeks we find them, tucked away in kitchen drawers and cupboards, behind books in the bookcase, in my husband's shoes. He takes one out of his house shoe and puts it under our daughter's pillow. Later, she is astonished to find it there. "I didn't put it there," she insists. "Who do you think did?" I ask. She looks at me for a long time. "A squirrel," she finally says, and I don't know if she really believes this or not. But I don't set her straight.

IN BRIEF

I wrote the briefs a dozen years ago, and I have forgotten most of them. I read them now like they're news once again. And once again, I gasp at the wickedness and misfortune in the world. I wonder what's happened to the people I wrote about. Did the criminals remain criminals? Does anyone remember the ones who died? I don't remember them. I learned about most of them talking on the phone to a police sergeant or public information officer.

I scan the *Crime and Fire Reports* briefs for April 29, 1997:

Infant not seriously hurt in wreck
Man pinned under truck
Woman set on fire
Fire at restaurant
Ex-boyfriend held in attack

The third headline catches my eye, and suddenly I remember it. I read the brief that I wrote:

A Victorville woman suffered second- and third-degree burns to 55 percent of her body Sunday after her ex-husband allegedly doused her with gasoline and set her on fire in front of children and other witnesses in the parking lot of a pizza parlor in the 17000 block of Valley Boulevard.

Police said Rialto resident Howard Streeter, 37, beat his ex-wife, 39-year-old Yolanda Butler, in the Chuck E. Cheese's parking lot shortly after 3 p.m. Sunday. Streeter then got a can of gasoline out of his car, poured it on Butler and set her on fire. Streeter, chased down by several witnesses, was arrested for mayhem, infliction of injury to spouse and other charges. A witness helped extinguish the fire before firefighters arrived.

OAK

I sit at the base of the oak, my back resting on its trunk, and try to imagine its roots, spreading beneath the grass. I cannot. I have learned that a mature oak might have five hundred million living root tips, and that its roots might reach an area four to seven times the width of the tree's crown.

I have now sat here right at the tree's base where it meets the grass so many times that my son, not yet two, has begun to mimic me. He, too, sits with his back resting against the trunk, experiencing it, taking it in. He has learned from his mother: this is what we do, we sit with trees.

IN BRIEF

I find a brief dated May 8, 1997, that reports that Yolanda Butler, the woman whose ex-husband set her on fire, died as a result of her injuries. And that is the end of the story of Yolanda Butler. I can find no more about her in my three-ring binder. The trail goes cold. I reread the two briefs. The preciseness of certain facts is chilling: *55 percent of her body, Chuck E. Cheese, doused with gasoline, in front of children.* And yet I cringe at the paucity of real information, of emotion. Why was I not outraged and heartbroken? I was not, I am sure, for my life went on as before, without a hitch. I hammered out the brief, and then, no doubt, picked up the phone to call another cop, to jovially say, "Hey, Corporal So-and-So, anything going on today in your neck of the woods?"

OAK

When I lived in Virginia, I knew another pin oak. This one was on the neighbor's lot but overhung our yard. All winter, it kept its brown leaves, shivering and rustling them, and I always thought, *I am like that tree,* or sometimes, *that tree is like me.* And then in spring, right before sending out its new leaves, it would finally, begrudgingly give up its previous year's leaves, and they would scuttle and scrape, a final rasp of autumn before spring, months after all the other leaves were gone, raked up into leaf bags. This is a common trait of certain pin oaks, I learn. Though they are deciduous, they keep their dead leaves until the new ones appear. Though not evergreen, the leaves are *persistent.*

I wonder if my new pin oak is persistent. I watch its leaves, waiting for the first hints of fall color. I wait to learn more. I wait to know it better. It takes years to get to know anyone, even—and perhaps especially—a tree.

IN BRIEF

The dearth of information, the bare-bones reporting, is a common feature of briefs. We reported what the police told us, and we didn't spend time contacting the families of victims or seeking out additional information. Some of the briefs are just a few sentences long.

In four sentences we learn that: a fifteen-year-old girl was shot dead while visiting friends; the shooter, who had been standing in the street, got in a car and drove away.

Two days later, another four sentences: A sixteen-year-old boy was arrested in the girl's death; no other explanations are offered.

Four sentences: An eighteen-year-old man died in a gang shooting.

Four sentences: A sixteen-year-old boy was hit by a train and killed.

OAK

Every day I walk on the bright striped hearts of oak that gave up their lives over sixty years ago but that endure beneath my feet in the floorboards of my house. Indeed, oak is all around me. Our country is made of oak, not just the thousands of hardwood floors and woodwork in old houses. The Declaration of Independence and the Constitution are written in iron-gall ink, most likely made from oak trees. And the famed hull of the USS *Constitution*—nicknamed "Old Ironsides"—is hard not because it is made of iron, but because it is made of oak. "For ten thousand years oak was the prime resource of what was to become the Western world," writes Logan. Acorn flour, houses, churches, ink, tanned leather, roofs, casks, and ships have been fashioned from parts of the oak tree.

IN BRIEF

I learned how to write a hard news story from an old-school journalist who believed his students needed to master the inverted pyramid before dabbling in New Journalism or feature writing. We practiced writing one news story after another, distilling the key facts and placing them at the top, and then adding information in the body of the story in descending order of importance. The idea was to give readers the most important information up front, in the lead. The idea was that readers aren't likely to read the whole story anyway; readers will skim and take the big news off the top like whipped cream off of cocoa, and only a small minority of them will ever read past a jump or get to the end of a news story, that thick murky sludge at the bottom of the cup. This practice served me well when it came to writing police briefs, which were still mostly written in the old, hard-news, inverted-pyramid style: tell the reader everything important up front.

A man riding a motorcycle without a helmet was killed Monday afternoon after a

*police pursuit when he crashed into the concrete base of a bridge over Interstate 10
near Mt. Vernon Avenue.*

*The pursuit began when a Colton police officer tried to pull over the man for
committing a traffic violation near Rancho Avenue and Johnston Street. The man
began to pull over to the curb as instructed, then suddenly took off, police said.*

*The man, whose name has not been released pending notification of next of
kin, reached speeds of more than 90 miles an hour on city streets. The officer followed behind but had to reduce his speed due to traffic.*

*As the victim tried to get on the I-10 at Mt. Vernon Avenue, he lost control
and crashed into the bridge base. He was taken to Loma Linda University Medical Center with head injuries, where he was pronounced dead on arrival.*

Perhaps the key information is contained in the first sentence, but by far
the most interesting sentence comes in the middle: *The man began to pull
over to the curb as instructed, then suddenly took off.* For that brief moment of
hesitation, he becomes human to me. I can see him there, at that juncture
where he made the decision, where the paths diverged: To surrender and
be charged with a crime? Or to flee? To select this life, or that one? And
he chose.

OAK

Our oak has anemia. We learn this during a preventive care appointment
with an arborist. He has come out to simply look at our trees, tell us what
he can. He points out the small holes that have been drilled in the trunk of
the oak where it has been treated for iron deficiency in the past. He likens
this to going to a doctor for a shot of vitamins in order to make up for a
deficient diet. He doesn't recommend such radical treatment.

We are to give coffee to the oak. This, apparently, will help with the
anemia, but not in a direct way: coffee grounds spread around the base will
encourage a wider spectrum of microorganisms, which will help enrich
the soil.

We learn that our tree lost its central leader, possibly in a storm. It
used to be an even bigger tree. There is a hole where the leader broke, and
the arborist is concerned. He can't tell how large it is from the ground.
It might be superficial, or it might go deep into the tree's center. He will
come back later with his climbing equipment and take a look.

IN BRIEF

In a brief titled, "Children removed from home," I wrote about five children, ages three through eight, who had been found covered in feces and eating dog food. The police sergeant I talked to called the home a "pigsty." I have seen pigsties, and I think it was something worse.

Sometimes there were just a couple briefs, and on other days, as many as ten or twelve. Often the other reporters would add briefs to the column if they got a bit of news while pursuing other stories. It was a collaborative effort. When I left at five or six in the evening, the night cops reporter would check back in with the police departments and sometimes add briefs. What appeared in the paper the next day was often news to me. I would read the additional briefs, thinking, so that's what happened while I was eating dinner, while I was brushing my teeth and putting on my nightgown. So that's the horror that was going on in the world while I was searching for the dental floss.

OAK

I cannot make use of the inverted pyramid to tell you of my oak. It bears no news, no tidings. Perhaps the earth whispers to it that autumn is approaching. The wind blows, the leaves prepare to crisp, the coursing of life in the trunk slows. When I write of the tree, my words are deflected by its corrugated bark. They fall short. The tree has no need for language, and yet I try to invent it and reinvent it in words.

I have known the tree for only a season. This is not nearly long enough.

IN BRIEF

When we learned that a homicide was gang related, it became a brief. But why? I wanted to know. I once asked the editor this question. "Because those people don't read the paper," he said, meaning the gang members, and the gangs members' families, and anyone who knew the gangs. We had an audience, and it dictated content. And it cared about rich, white college boys who died in bar fights, about department store heiresses who were dragged to death during carjackings, about mansions that went up in smoke, but not about dead gang members, dead homeless, dead nameless.

A worker sweeping a parking lot found a body wrapped in a bedspread Friday morning in an alley behind an apartment complex in the 1000 block of Mount

Vernon Avenue. The man, a young Hispanic male, who has not been identified, had been shot once in the upper body, police said.

Why did I believe it necessary to collect fat binders full of these fragments of ruined lives? Why do I keep them still? In most cases, the two or four sentences I wrote were my entire tribute to a human being to whom something atrocious had happened. If the police never learned more, if another reporter did the follow-up, if there was nothing to add, I was finished. The trail ended. Rarely did we run another brief to say: the police still know nothing, the killer is still at large, the victim is still dead. But sometimes we did.

Police are still trying to identify a young Hispanic man who was found dead last week in an alley in the 1100 block of Mount Vernon Avenue.

The man, who was about 5 feet, 8 inches tall and weighed 140 pounds, was found wrapped in a bedspread early Friday morning. The man, found wearing only a pair of blue jeans, had been shot once in the upper torso.

Police believe he was killed in another location and moved to the alley between 6 and 10 hours after his death. The man was between 19 and 25 years old and had a thin mustache.

He also had a tattoo on the upper left portion of his chest. It was about 10 inches high and showed a person's face in profile with a tear on the cheek and the words "El Ruben."

And in the case of this unidentified man, we ran a third plea for information, a month later. We repeated the same information, though the police had revised his size to 5 feet, 6 inches, and 120 pounds. I quoted a police lieutenant: "We've gone nowhere with this. We have nothing. . . . We need someone to come to us and say, 'Hey, that looks like my old neighbor.' We're looking for any leads at this point." We even ran a police sketch of the dead man: the generic face of someone I might have passed on the street, indeed, someone who might have once been my neighbor, if only I paid attention to my neighbors. I think he *was* my neighbor, in one sense. And I never came forward to claim him as my own. And as far as I know, no one else did either. His trail ends here in my clips.

OAK

In some forests, Logan writes, oak trees of the same species graft their roots together and "become one flesh." Through their shared root system, the stronger, dominant trees may provide the weaker trees with nutrients.

In this way, even the roots of stumps can continue to live and contribute to the forest: "The grafted roots may go on acquiring water and nutrients for the surviving trees long after their parent tree has rotted away."

IN BRIEF

Two men stole six cases of baby food at gunpoint at a local grocery store. The details in the brief are as spare as always, and yet the subtext aches with its own life. The untold story is bursting at the seams of those three compact sentences that tell you who, what, when, where, how—but not why. I can almost hear the baby's wails, the mother's pleas from between the sooty lines of newspaper text. And instead of saying, *Catch these criminals and put them in jail,* why don't we say, *Please come forward and we will help you?* There has to be another way.

OAK

One morning my daughter sees the neighbor girls standing by the trunk of the oak and poking it with their fingers. She charges outside, shouting, "Hey, that's our tree! Don't hurt our tree!" even though the girls are her friends. She is protective of the tree, has claimed it as her own. I know she has probably learned this attitude from me, though I have not yet been shouting at the neighbors, about trees or anything else.

IN BRIEF

Violence and death were all around me. Every day I walked through a minefield, and miraculously, I had avoided all the mines. It was a matter of time, of luck. I had to be vigilant. The criminals were everywhere. The man walking across the parking lot was likely a carjacker, so I hurried up and started my car. The man in the Taco Bell was a rapist, so I'd better not stop there. My life would end in an accident on the interstate, so I'd better not drive there. Better to take the surface streets. But maybe that would be my mistake: maybe I'd wrap my car around a eucalyptus tree. Maybe an elderly woman would run a light and kill me. Safer to take the interstate after all. Safer yet to call in sick. But what if an intruder came to kill me? What if I fell and hit my head on the kitchen counter in a freak accident? Safer to go to work, to be lulled by the static of the police scanner. Safer to learn of the misfortunes of others. Because if I knew about all the crime in the world, maybe nothing would happen to me. If I paid enough attention, wrote enough briefs, I wouldn't become a police brief myself.

OAK

The squirrels pelt acorns at us out of the tree. They bury them in the grass. Acorns are beguiling; I can see why my daughter and the squirrels collect them. I can see why they are compelled to move them from place to place. My husband etches a face on one with his fingernail, the cap serving as a beret, and says with a bad French accent, "I am zee Frenchman Jean-Claude Pierre."

The acorns keep turning up. I find one in the pocket of my old fleece sweater that I wear around the house all fall and winter. It is small and striped, unlike the larger, monochrome acorns that our pin oak produces. A vagrant has made its way into my pocket. I don't remember putting it there. The trees are doing their work.

Later, once I have grown attached to my pocket acorn, I reach in to feel its familiar smooth shape, and it's gone. The trees are doing their work.

IN BRIEF

One time a seventeen-year-old girl was pulled over and given a ticket for following behind a highway patrol car too closely. "Eight minutes later," my brief reads, "she lost control of her 1986 Toyota Corolla, hit the center divider and rolled. She was pronounced dead at the scene." At the time of the accident, she had been driving in excess of one hundred miles per hour.

And I can see it all, thanks to those eight minutes. I can imagine the sudden anger that spread through her limbs like a disease, the erratic thoughts: How dare he give her a ticket? How the hell was she going to explain this to her father? I can feel her stepping hard, and harder yet, on the accelerator, her adrenaline rushing, going faster and faster, perhaps not even glancing at the speedometer, weaving in and out of traffic. She would show him. She would drive off the face of the world; this was her way of flipping the bird to the trooper who pulled her over, to authority. I could have been that girl. Maybe I once was that girl. Actually, I had once driven my car one hundred miles per hour, just to see if it would go that fast. Actually, I had, as a teenager, had a run-in with the police. Actually, I think I was that girl. But I was luckier.

I couldn't continue being all those people. I couldn't lead all those lives. I couldn't keep dying so many deaths. There had to be another way. And writing those briefs—those sound bites of bad news, those sudden, unrelenting jabs of destruction coming from all sides—I just couldn't see another way.

OAK

The arborist recommends we plant another oak in the front yard. I'd like to think the root systems of the two trees will meet, grapple, cohere. The younger, more vigorous tree will help support the older oak, prolonging its life. And later, when the older oak is dead, the younger tree will continue to benefit from its affiliation with the gone tree's prolific root system. They will help each other. They will both live longer in companionship. This can be true of trees as well as people.

IN BRIEF

A thirteen-year-old boy accidentally shot himself while watching the Super Bowl. I could picture him all too clearly, watching the game, twiddling the gun, like a toy, in the nervous way that some boys have, their hands always needing to be active, engaged. I have known boys like that. I have known that boy.

Death was coming out of the woodwork. Who are all these people dying and being murdered? I developed a low-grade daily terror of going to work, of what I might learn there. I developed a terror of speaking to the families of victims. Once I had to approach the mother of a young man whose throat had been slashed. Intruding into her grief seemed morally wrong, an outrage, and yet in my line of work, I knew I would be asked to commit it, again and again.

One day I was sent to the hospital to find the family of children who had been badly burned in a fire and were being treated in the burn unit. For half an hour, I just sat in the hospital parking lot. Finally I walked into the lobby and then turned around and walked out again because, simply, I could not bear to talk to the family of these children, to peer into their sorrow like a peeping tom, creeping from one window of grief to another. I returned to the office and told my editor, "I did not find the family," which was true. I didn't tell him that I hadn't even looked. I should have known then, but I let it continue. I went to work and cringed at the scanner noise and wrote more briefs.

OAK

There is news today: the leaves have started to change, the green beginning to marble with yellow. The oak is preparing for winter, and so should I, whatever that means in the twenty-first century. Find the Polartec fleece, make sure the storm windows are shut, buy a jug of lotion for dry skin, replenish the Earl Grey tea, set the thermostat to sixty-eight, plan soups, press leaves in books for winter crafts, put flannel sheets on the beds, take the car to the mechanic for winterization, make some hot chocolate and learn to sit still indoors with a book.

IN BRIEF

Hell was the unending mutter of the police scanner. Hell was the dozen phone calls I had to make, asking again and again: What's going on today? Translation: Who has been murdered this time? What heinous crime can you tell me about? Hell was walking up to a woman whose son had been murdered and asking her what her son was like. Did he like sports cars and golf, mystery novels and mountain climbing, single-malt whiskey and walking his dog? Was he kind and funny, smart and affectionate, devoted and handsome, gifted and outgoing, clever and strong? How could he be otherwise?

One time a burglar entered a house through a sliding glass door. A woman who was asleep on the living room couch said hello to the intruder. The man was so startled that he ran away.

Annie Dillard wrote in *Teaching a Stone to Talk*, "What is the difference between a cathedral and a physics lab? Are they not both saying: Hello?"

I like to think that an energetic, friendly voice shouting out "Hello!" to the burglar made the hair on his neck stand up. Here was another human being who recognized him as human, worthy of a greeting. She didn't leap up in fear or scream or shout, "What are you doing here?" or "I'm calling the police!" She said: "Hello," a greeting to life, the universe. Whatever or whoever you are, she said, I recognize you as worthy of a hello. Hello!

And all of my police briefs: just shouts of "hello!" And there are better ways, I think, to greet the cosmos.

OAK

The leaves, spotted yellow and brown, have started to fall, though most still cleave to the tree. In *The Life of an Oak*, Glenn Keator writes that an oak leaf has its characteristic indentations between lobes to "allow bits of light to pass through and be absorbed by a lobe on a leaf just below, like a jigsaw-puzzle." Even the leaves look out for one another.

My daughter brings me handfuls of leaves plucked out of our lawn, but some are aberrant. One is the glossy green of summer, another is cardinal red. I can't believe they've come from our tree. All I can see are yellow and brown in its canopy. But the jigsaw-puzzle lobes are unmistakable. My daughter asks me to save all the leaves for her. Later, she brings me more. We have leaves scattered all over the house. We slip some into books, at random. Others wither and curl on the kitchen counter, on the bookcase. She asks me for the leaf she found yesterday. I offer her one. "Not *that* one," she insists. "The one I found in the *afternoon* with Gramp, not the one I found in the *morning*." She keeps tabs on her leaves. The missing leaf is never found, and is, apparently, irreplaceable. "There is no other leaf like it," she insists. And, of course, she is right.

Most of the leaves still cling tenaciously to the tree. I watch them. Every day, I take stock. I wait for the tree to show me what will come next.

IN DEPTH

I once wrote a story about a young man named Homero Vargas who was found stuffed in a fifty-gallon trash can behind a house. He had died of a gunshot wound. I think one of the reasons he was not just a brief but worthy of thirteen inches and a mug shot is that he had played football at a prominent high school in town. I talked to his former football coach, who called him a "solid boy," and the crime "a sad waste of a good boy." He might have been a brief, but for that. And had he been a brief—worthy of just four sentences—what happened next would not have followed.

Several weeks after the story ran, a man came in the newsroom and asked for me. He walked to my desk and he looked at me. I had never seen him before.

"My name is Jesus Vargas," he finally said to me. "You wrote a story about my son, Homero." He sat down across from me, took my hand, and held it. He looked at me intently and paused to control his voice. "I want to thank you so much for this wonderful story about my son," he said. I saw that he carried with him a creased copy of the newspaper where the story appeared.

I didn't know what to say. I could see that what he was doing—in coming to see me—was both very difficult and very important.

"Homero was a good boy," he said. He spoke with an accent. He went on to tell me about his son's strong faith, his dedication to the Seventh-day Adventist Church. He spoke about his son playing football and working at a construction company after high school. Mostly, I listened and waited for the man to leave. *I didn't do your son justice,* I wanted to say. *I didn't know him.* Homero Vargas had been twenty, and I myself had just turned twenty-three. And this life was about to end, but I didn't know it then.

Before he left, Jesus Vargas stood and held the newspaper tightly to his chest. "I just wanted to say thank you for this," he said. "I love you for this." And before I could respond, he was gone.

I love you for this. I cringed at the words. I did not deserve love for this. This was not what I wanted to be loved for, not even close.

Homero Vargas might have been a brief, and had he been a brief, I wouldn't have talked to his football coach, and my name wouldn't have appeared on my story. And his father wouldn't have come to see me. How much of the world was I closing off to myself, writing those dozens upon hundreds of briefs?

After Jesus Vargas left, I saw that I could have written a better story about his son after talking to him, but I also saw that it wouldn't have been good enough. I saw that my attempts—the attempts that newspapers make in reporting the news—were inadequate in really knowing a person and the meaning of his death. I could ask Jesus Vargas a thousand questions. I could write fifty inches, a hundred inches. It would never be sufficient.

Instead, I wrote a column. I wrote about Jesus Vargas coming to see me and the difficulties in maintaining empathy as a police reporter. I wrote about the challenges of compressing a life into a tight news story. My editor chose the title "Bringing Homero Vargas back to life" for my column, though that is not really what my column was about. If only words had that power. They fall short of the mark. Homero Vargas was and is forever beyond their reach. He deflects my attempts. I cannot reinvent him.

At the end of my column, I wrote that I could still be moved by others' grief. And I concluded: "May I never lose that." A month later, I left newspapers for good. And I hope that I haven't lost it.

I love you for this, he said to me, baring himself before leaving. He meant the words as a blessing, and they have followed me for years. But at the time, they did not feel like a blessing.

I love you for this. I watch my children run under the tree. We wait for the arborist to return. He will climb into our tree and peer into its heart, see the damage there. He will tell us how deep the wound is. *I love you for this.*

Mulberry

THE MULBERRY LEAVES I carried in a shoe box to my first-grade classroom were my proof that I could nurture life. Those of us who could procure the leaves were given a batch of silkworms to take home and raise. The bristly black inchlings transmogrified into fat white slugs that munched leaves ceaselessly in their shoe-box home. Did they covet freedom? I was too transfixed with their insatiable progress to free them, and then one day they began contorting and writhing, spinning themselves into privacy, into a sleep like death from which they emerged as leathery white moths, flopping and thrashing against the cardboard. Finally I released them outdoors, returning them to the natural world where I assumed they belonged, hoping that they would live as they were meant to, believing in my six-year-old heart that no creature should be held captive.

In sixth grade a girl named Sarah told me that her hobby was tree climbing: not stamp collecting or knitting, not anything that left a tangible mark in the world. Intrigued, I decided I would become a tree climber too. With two fruitless mulberries and a massive fruited one to ascend, I splayed myself high in branches, held aloft in rough brown arms, up to the sun and the wind, as though the trees were offering me up, as though I was the treasure they had plucked up to hold out in their chaffed hands. And I reached with them, for light and warmth and life, for wind, for sustenance, for rain, gorging on purple berries along with the shrieking birds.

That same sixth-grade year, my period arrived. Messy and pointless, it had nothing to do with my life as a tree climber. I secured a pad in my underwear and climbed, descending only at dusk with hands stained purple.

✳

At fifteen my body, poised like a question mark, sought out a new purpose, asking: And am I alluring? And what can I do? To find out, I snuck out at night to meet a boy. January air seeping through my open window alerted my parents. They shut and locked the window, capturing me outside with my crime. Finding my window locked and dreading the grimness of that coming dawn, I rested against the trunk of a fruitless mulberry. It offered no warmth, no softness, but were it not there, were I left in the starkness of an empty yard, I would have been more forsaken.

I might have climbed it, ensnaring myself in its branches, misunderstood, mildly drunk, stranded in a winter night, forsaken by parents who believed my motives sinister, a boy who didn't realize a whole complicated, ripe person burst within me. To be discovered in a tree was a point I wanted to make. The tree would have pinned me to the sky, a star made flesh, mounting me in my natural setting. I wanted most to escape my body, to transcend it, but it held me forever captive to the earth.

Instead of climbing, I only looked up at a branch like an elbow, crooked out as though waiting for another tree to hook on and swing your partner. I was not alone, though I did not think of the tree as a presence so much as an absence of absence. In my memory, the tree is there, though much of the rest of that night is not. The tree's permanence mars my memory, etching itself, in a way that the constant flight of people and emotions cannot. The tree is there, but my parents and the boy especially remain as hardly more than ghosts.

✳

Fifteen years and fifteen hundred miles away, seeing for the first time the purple glints of my newborn's eyes, her skin downy and puckered and tumescent, perfectly ripe for this world, I thought again of mulberries, of being held in their branches, of purple stains, of the burst of berry on tongue, and I saw giving birth was akin to climbing a tree: a reaching toward light, nourishment, endurance, life, a cradling and an offering of the most cherished to the world.

Maybe this is not true. Maybe I did not think of the mulberry then. Maybe I seamed it into my memory later: mulberry, birth. Who can say what thoughts occur during birth? It is stark physicality, a rending. It is an elbow against sky. And yet, on some level, the mulberry was there, subsumed by my laboring. Everything in my life was there with me, on that delivery table. Is it a lie to create memories after the fact? Is it a fiction to plaster over experience with words? Is it a violence to insist a tree means something other than itself?

My daughter's birth will mean a thousand different things as she becomes her different selves. Now it means mulberry, and she likes that. Significance accrues only in hindsight, one filament spun out at a time, encasing the moment, hiding it from light, from danger, the only way we know to preserve memories, to nurture them. We become ourselves through stories. And our stories are the cocoons that gently hold the things that cannot be uttered.

I tell my daughter about raising silkworms and climbing mulberries, but I do not tell her how I watched my liberated moths flounder stupidly in the dust until I finally turned my back on their suffering and ultimate death, implicit in creating creatures that had no place in the world. I do not tell her what I learned years later: that domesticated silkworms do not live in the wild, that we have made them what they are and they live only in our captivity. I do not tell her that cocoons are boiled to kill the worms and make the silk easier to work. I do not tell her that to be born from its cocoon the moth ruins the silk, and besides all that, the moths cannot fly.

This daughter of mine, almost silkworm-raising age, announces her plans: after her moths hatch and fly away, she will collect their silk for her grandmother to knit her a sweater.

Yes, I lie. *That's a beautiful idea*, I add.

Will I climb a mulberry tree someday, too?

Yes, I tell her. *You will climb a mulberry tree someday, too.* And I hope it is not a lie.

We hold one another captive, she and I. And one day I will release her. But our mother-daughter captivity, she will discover, is only the first of many.

Navel Country

(But where is what I started for, so long ago?
And why is it yet unfound?)
  —WALT WHITMAN, "FACING WEST FROM CALIFORNIA'S SHORES"

Riverside, California, circa 1979

We hurtle down the narrow road in Grandpa's Ford LTD, whistling cleanly through the orange trees, the dark green foliage whipping past. Up ahead, the leaves all seem a jumble, but looking directly out my open window, I see the neat rows opening up, the cleaving of soil between the evenly spaced trees. For a split second, each row lines up straight in my line of sight, and then the next supersedes it, and the next, and the next, each one a clean part in the land. Zip-zip-zip-zip, the rows whip past with an even tempo, a corresponding music in the whoosh-whoosh-whooshing of the leaves.

We're headed up to the ranch, barreling along Palmyrita Avenue in an enormous mint-green two door with automatic windows. I'm small on the big bench seat, skittering back and forth with the turns, clawing at the vinyl to keep from careening into Grandpa. He's a fast, aggressive driver. The trees keep flying past until he slows and pulls onto a dirt road running between two groves. Creeping along it, he vigilantly peers down the rows on either side, looking for anything out of the ordinary, for trouble. Suddenly he turns the steering wheel, plunging the car right down one of the narrow rows, forcing it in, and we are riding in a wedge that passes through the trees, branches scraping on both sides. I shrink away from the foliage erupting in through my open window, the trees seeming to be clambering into the car with me. Their glossy leaves fall on my lap, and occasionally an orange thuds to the floorboard. The car's antenna bounces crazily, springing off branches. Grandpa rests his left arm on the open window, never moving, not even flinching when a branch scratches his tan skin. He's impervious to these unruly trees because he's the lord of this vast kingdom of citrus; as far as I know, he very nearly rules the world.

❦

Looking down from the Box Springs Mountains, the orange groves are needlepoint, an elaborate embroidering upon the land. Dark green burrs set at regular intervals, the trees are globular, their full branches skirting the ground, their shiny ovate leaves present year round, unchanging but for the cycle of fruit: the saccharine blossoms, the small green fruit, and finally, the brilliant ripeness of temperate winter. January in a navel grove is a page from a storybook. The leaves seem to be a setting, a dark green satin, to display the gleaming jewels of fruit. Orange is both a color and a fruit. No other fruit can quite manage it; peach and lemon, raspberry and watermelon are shades of colors, not colors proper, not members of the rainbow. But an orange *is* orange. And I feel proud, that we—this country, my family—own this color, that it is ours and that it is tangible and edible and I can cup it in my hand.

Brown and dusty most of the year, the Box Springs Mountains are covered in scrub with a few sycamores growing deep in gullies, the highest peak just three thousand feet. Farther off are the real mountains, the San Bernardino and San Gabriel Ranges, blue and purple, snowcapped, over eleven thousand feet at the highest peak, an ornate backdrop to our life in navel country—except that on many days, the mountains don't seem to be there at all, invisible for weeks behind a shroud of smog, so that when they suddenly reappear on a clear day, it's as if they've been unrolled from the sky, Hollywood scenery tacked up along the horizon to make our life idyllic. The smog is never idyllic, brownish orange and thick, pooling up in valleys, obstructing views and lungs. The startling splendor alternates with long strings of smog-alert days, when the air quality is so poor that we're kept in at recess and PE, so that we won't physically exert ourselves and breathe in even more of the toxic air. We sustain ourselves on tiny sips of air, waiting for the mountains to rematerialize, waiting to breathe.

Everything I know about the history of citrus I learn by looking at historic fruit-crate labels. Here are the stories, the sun-drenched groves, the sun-kissed misses offering up fruit, the lavender mountain ranges in the distance. This is what life had once been like every single day, long before I arrived on the scene to a smog-choked, congested city approaching two hundred thousand residents. I wait for those rare, pristine days when the view outside and the picture on the label briefly correspond, the landscapes aligning. When the mountains look like a blessing on the trees, when I glimpse the juicy sections of a navel gaping apart in a woman's slim hand, when I hold up an orange to azure sky and imagine that even I could grace a citrus crate, I am living in that storybook landscape, a life worthy of framing. Only vestiges of that true life remain, just twinges I feel now and then, a sudden spasm of nostalgia, an aftershock of paradise.

The actual history behind these images is opaque to me; I know that the "parent" navel tree sits in a cage at a busy intersection in town, but in what way a tree can be a parent I don't understand. The pieces of the story I hear seem to be scattered over the globe. In the 1820s in Brazil, a mutation caused a tree to produce sweet seedless oranges with a navel, an embryonic orange, a conjoined twin that the larger twin absorbs into itself. Because all navel oranges are sterile, they can be reproduced only via grafting—joining budstock from the parent tree to rootstock of another tree—and thus all navel trees are clones, genetically identical to one another. In *Oranges*, John McPhee calls the navel orange "a kind of monster." This monster eventually made its way to Washington, D.C., where it was propagated and christened the Washington Navel. Meanwhile, in 1870, John W. North recruited a group of eastern families to start a colony, Riverside, in Southern California. Among the first settlers was Eliza Tibbets, who had once lived next door to Department of Agriculture botanist William Saunders in Washington. He sent his former neighbor a couple of the navel seedlings, which she planted on her Riverside homestead and—as the myth goes— watered with dirty dishwater. Riverside's climate proved ideal for the fruit, and quickly the "large, open, treeless plain" (as Charles Nordhoff, an early travel writer, described the area in 1874) was transformed into navel country: groomed rows of verdant trees as far as the eye could see. By 1895, just a little over two decades after Tibbets planted her trees and began sharing their cuttings, Riverside had the highest per capita income in the country due largely to that monstrous, sterile tree: the navel orange.

In 1922, when my grandfather was six years old, he moved with his family from Tennessee to La Verne, California. According to notes made by my aunt, when my grandfather graduated from high school in 1933, "he already had ten seasons of weeding and pruning and pulling out bad trees and putting in new trees and cultivating and furrowing and irrigating and fumigating and gophering and loading and hauling and driving teams of horses and mules and tractors by working for his father after school, Saturdays, and summers, except during football season." The following year, the family moved to Riverside, where my grandfather eventually became the big boss at both Natoco Groves, which at one time managed several thousand acres of fruit, and National Orange Company, which packed and shipped the fruit. In the Depression and war and early housing-boom years, it was said that Riverside was a place where men swapped orange groves the way their grandfathers did horses. My grandfather was constantly "trading up," getting better and larger groves, securing his portion of the citrus empire. He devoted more than seventy years of his life to the citrus industry.

"This is navel country," my grandfather said in an interview for *The Press-Enterprise* in 1979, more than a century after Tibbets planted her trees. "Many people insist on planting other varieties when it's been proved this area is best suited for navels." As a child, I have a keen sense that we have perfected the land—or at least my forebears have. When I feel that twinge—when I enter the orange-crate label—the landscape is so beautiful I believe it to be natural and enduring. It stretches indefinitely into the past and the future. It stretches across the land in vast swaths, but what I don't fully understand is that it was once even more immense, lapping to the edges of this world like an endless, burled green sea; what I don't know is that already it has been eaten up by developers, that it is vanishing almost before my very eyes.

❧

Riverside, California, circa 1979

Grandpa stops the car and we get out. He heads off down one of the rows, and I follow, keeping an even distance between us, watching his bowlegged cowboy swagger. He stops at the wind machine—a propeller mounted atop a tower fifty feet off the ground—and talks to one of his men, who is tinkering with the engine that sits on a concrete pad nestled in the trees. I hang back and watch. Grandpa's a big man, easily six feet tall, with a big tight gut like a hard round melon that swells the inside of his shirt, resting on his belt. He wears pale-colored Wranglers, tan or light blue, and short-sleeved, Western-style snap-front shirts. He smokes a Winston while he talks to the man, one of the ranch hands.

I play demurely within sight, running up and down the rows, jumping off standpipes, scampering under trees, picking snails off trunks, examining the rusty orchard heaters in which the smudging crews used to burn oil to battle frost. Grandpa likes having me on the peripheries, unobtrusive. He tells people I'm his little granddaughter just recently over from Russia. As the first grandchild, I am, to adapt a cliché, the orange of his eye. He desires an affectionate, loving granddaughter, but I am quiet and introverted, fearful of his booming voice, his barks and outbursts, his calluses and rough edges, the scratches on his arm made by tree branches.

When he's done talking, I follow him to the immense avocado tree that I call my schoolhouse. We enter the tree like a solemn room, the branches sweeping the ground on all sides, the walls and ceiling glowing green. Grandpa lifts me up onto the branch that's my usual perch, and I begin to teach him, in my hybrid Russian-English. The Russian is slowly being erased from my speech, the English taking over, growing wild like an invasive plant, but my native Russian still persists in words here, phrases there. I don't actually know what language I'm speaking. Even though it's two languages cobbled together, to me it seems to be just one. It is simply a string of the words I know, put in a sequence that best conveys my meaning. Either Grandpa can't hear me, or he can't understand what I'm saying—or both. He lets me prattle on, barking, "Is that right?" and "You don't say!" at random intervals.

The lesson over, we head back to the car. On our way out of the grove Grandpa stops at his corrugated metal shed to put cat food out for the feral cats. There are always strays up here, cats and often dogs that get dumped by people who don't want them anymore. The groves are near the county dump, so people are always dumping unwanted stuff up here. Broken-backed sofas, bent floor lamps, and black bags full of amorphous, foul-smelling garbage are often heaped in the ditches on the side of the road.

�֍

"I'm heading up to the ranch," Grandpa says. But now these words are a call to my brother Alex. Five years younger, he has colonized Grandpa's heart. It's become clear to me that a grandson is what Grandpa wanted all along. I have been only an adequate stand-in until the grandson was ripe, ready to head off to the ranch. Alex enters Grandpa's world more fully than I ever did. Together they laugh at belches and at women's big butts. They make jokes about their "peckers" and play pull my finger endlessly and guffaw about busting wind. They mock the silliness and artsy-fartsy ways of girls.

We've taken sides. I'm now in Grandma Bea's camp. I go with her to the antique stores and the horse races. Together we collect Madame Alexander dolls and Cabbage Patch Kids. In the evenings we watch *Dynasty* and *Falcon Crest*. She hides out from Grandpa, sewing and painting and watching television. She tells me he's a tyrant, impossible to live with. He never allows her to spend enough, to buy the things she wants. She squirrels away some of the grocery money to buy dolls and furniture. I am the locus of many of her efforts; she sews a closetful of clothes for me and gives me dozens of dolls. Sometimes I feel that she has been waiting decades for my arrival. She needs a girl in her life. She has five sons. Her only daughter is in a mental institution.

Eventually the old farmhouse and its five acres are sold to developers. Bea angles to get an old dilapidated Victorian to renovate, to fill with antiques and dolls. Going behind her back, Grandpa buys a sprawling country-club ranch house with a pool. Bea mutters the word *divorce*. She says Grandpa will outlive her and she'll never get her hands on the money. She tells me, again and again, that he's a tyrant. "Why don't you divorce him?" I finally ask. "Because we aren't the kind of people who do things like that," she says. "And he'd keep all the money, leave me with nothing." Bea keeps a bedroom for me in her new house. It's filled with dolls.

Grandpa hands out money to me when the mood strikes him, and every birthday and Christmas I receive a one-hundred-dollar bill tucked into a card signed in Bea's hand: *Love, Grandpa*. I believe that in having a miniscule window on his life, I know all about him. I believe that he's always been this same man, old and fat, rich and volatile. That he lived nearly six decades before I was born, that he did not always have spare bills to hand out to little girls doesn't occur to me. I believe him to be indescribably wealthy and stingy. I believe he has a wallet bloated with money, and it's unfair that its dispersal is entirely contingent on the vacillations of his moods. I'm ignorant of the history, of the Great Depression when he grew to manhood, of the years of saving, of his decades of work. He didn't hand out ten-dollar bills like oranges plucked from a tree to his own children. He didn't indulge them at all; quite the opposite.

I get a lot, but Alex gets more: more money, more trips to the ranch, shrimp for dinner. When I meekly ask if my sister Natasha and I can have some shrimp, Grandpa barks, "No! There isn't enough to go around. I got it for Alex." Natasha and I eat the shrimp tails left on Alex's plate, and I stew over the injustice of it. It's because we're girls—and we aren't sweet and beautiful and dainty girls. We're big and hungry girls. We're girls who bully our little brother. Later, after the shrimp tails are gone, Grandpa slips Natasha and me each a ten, his atonement. I take his money, but I don't forgive him. I have a simmering contempt for him, but I always take his money. I'm enraged that there are things girls can't do, language girls can't hear, jokes that aren't for girls' ears, that we're expected to be docile and satisfied with a spending allowance doled out to us to cover groceries and lipstick. I don't want to live in Grandpa's world. I belong in another world. One day, I will escape.

In the meantime, I punish Alex for being a boy. I dunk him in my grandparents' new pool until he beaches himself on the concrete, coughing up water. I fill his mouth with WHOPPERS while he sleeps. I kick him in the shin with a steel-toed boot. And yet, I can't help but like him. In the summer we stay up all night playing Nintendo, watching *Auntie Mame* on network television, waiting for the first seep of light on the horizon. Right before dawn, we set out, walking to the trailhead just a couple of blocks from our house. Together we climb Sugarloaf, the two-thousand-foot peak on the northwestern edge of Box Springs, just as the sun is coming up, watching out for rattlesnakes among the boulders and vegetation. When we reach the top, we look down over the other side into Highgrove and Grand Terrace, at the stretches of groves that Grandpa manages and the ones he owns. Maybe he's even down there somewhere, scraping his new white Mustang through the tight rows of trees, looking for vandals, checking his standpipes. We head back down the mountain, walking to the nearby strip mall to buy a dozen doughnut holes for seventy-five cents before going home to sleep the day away.

During the school year, Grandpa picks me up from middle school to drive me home. Our conversations on those ten-minute rides go nowhere. I wish he would just keep his mouth shut.

"How was school?" he barks.

"I don't know."

Silence.

"You still gettin' all them As?"

"I don't know."

More silence.

"You think you're smart enough to go to college? Huh?"

I don't reply.

"What do you want to go to college for anyway?"

"I don't know."

"Well what *do* you know?"

"I don't know."

"You should get married, stay home, and raise kids. That's what you should do. You'd make someone a nice wife."

I'm silent the rest of the way home. Maybe he expects me to argue with him, but I'm not that feisty. When I show him my report card with straight As, he pulls out his wallet. "You think you're so smart," he says snidely, handing me a fifty.

The trees keep disappearing, but I hardly notice. The process is gradual, insidious. What's a grove here, a grove there? One by one in my memory the groves vanish—they're there and then abruptly gone—the land suddenly denuded. In my child's mind there are no explanations for these sudden negations, these annihilations; there are no negotiations or land deals, and there is hardly even chronology. Simply one day you ride in a car and look out a window and where the groves used to be is empty land, or, if you look closely, not quite empty: oranges still litter the plowed ground, shaken loose by the violent wrenching of trees, the fruit telling me that very recently something cataclysmic occurred to several thousand trees. The oranges do not remain long. They shrink, turn brown, collapse, and vanish. The navel landscape is gradually written over, becoming first an empty field, and later a housing development or strip mall. In a year or two, I will not be able to say which groves came out in which order. I will not even be able to say whether my memory is accurate in superimposing ghostly trees over new subdivisions, whether all the places my mind puts trees were indeed once part of navel country. As more and more houses appear, I mentally populate the land with more and more trees, restoring it to what I believe is its natural state.

Riverside, California, circa 1979

Grandpa pulls up at the packing house, a long building that stretches along railroad tracks with loading docks and a false front. National Orange Company, *reads the sign on top.* Sunkist. Oranges. Grapefruit. *This is part of his domain, too. Grandpa's the big boss everywhere he goes. Two of my uncles work here, Ray running the office and Jeff on the packing-house floor.*

First we check on the packing. I am stunned by the whirring and clacking and chirruping of all the machines, the oranges bumping and jostling their way along the conveyors as though in a hurry, as though each is personally invested in its journey to New York or Omaha or Hong Kong. I can't follow the sequence of steps that occur here: the culling, the bathing, the waxing, the grading, the packing, the shipping. The machinery and noise overwhelm me. The packers are mostly women, and they're quick with their hands, packing a box of oranges in thirty-five to seventy seconds, depending on the size of the fruit. Grandpa walks the floor, sizing up the operation, pausing to speak to workers. Silently I shadow him.

We head to the office, a quieter, narrow room on one end of the building with three desks—one for Grandpa, one for Ray, and one for the secretary. Taking his place at his desk, Grandpa starts talking to Ray, busy working on a calculator. I sit in one of the wooden chairs along the wall and crane my neck to look at the framed orange-crate labels hanging above me. Grandpa talks about politics, about Reagan's bid for the presidency, and Ray periodically says, "Mmm-hmm," or "Is that right?" Grandpa likes to tell long, rambling stories that don't seem to have a point, or that have punch lines so amusing that he starts laughing before he's even reached the conclusion.

"The irrigation ditches were hand dug in them days," he's saying. "I can tell you anecdotes and stories about that for as long as you want to listen. Cap Lunderman, for one. They were digging a ditch for a pipeline up through there, and Cap come up—he was from Missouri, had a little old cigar there—and he was looking at that ditch—and every ranch has some guy that's a little bit goofy between the ears—and so Cap looked at that and said, 'Who dug that crooked part there?' And all the guys, they jumped on and blamed this one guy, and old Cap with that little old cigar—he took a little drag on it and says, 'What the hell's the rest of you been doing?'" Grandpa launches into his terrifying belly laugh, and then sputters out his conclusion: "In other words, the whole damn ditch was crooked!"

※

I develop the deep, aching nostalgia that afflicts those of us who are nostalgic not for times and places from our own pasts, but for times and places from our forebears' pasts, for imagined pasts that we ourselves never inhabited. My nostalgia becomes subsumed by dissatisfaction and, eventually, angst. The fact that Riverside's best days are behind it only means that there's nothing left for me. I live in a Riverside of gangs and smog, of delinquent kids who run wild in subdivisions while their parents commute three hours a day to jobs in Orange County or LA. I live in the Riverside that's one hour from anything worthwhile: the beach, the mountains, the desert, LA, Disneyland—Riverside being a *nowhere* that's only near *somewhere*. My Riverside rhymes with *homicide* and *suicide*. I'm stranded in an oasis with a perfect Mediterranean climate, marooned among cactus gardens and palm trees, shopping malls and housing developments, smog alerts and earthquakes, a fake mission and snarls of freeways headed in every direction, and disappearing orange groves.

I live in the Riverside that's part of the despicable Inland Empire, a monstrous, amorphous sprawl of tract homes and strip malls and pavement swallowing up large swaths of Riverside and San Bernardino Counties—in short, all the unhip inland regions east of LA and Orange Counties. The kids I go to school with at John W. North High School don't come from orange groves, from citrus. They're stoners, Goths, punks, skaters, athletes, gangbangers, and nerds, but they're not farmers. Riverside is, in our parlance, lame. We suffer a mild form of self-loathing for living in this armpit of America, a foul place that has some of the dirtiest air and worst traffic in the nation. We have inferiority complexes. Who, outside of Southern California, has ever even heard of Riverside? It's gritty and unglamorous. We clamor to get out. A boy at school boasts of getting drunk in Evergreen Cemetery and pissing on John W. North's grave, which I believe to be a brilliant expression of our feelings toward John W. North High School and, more generally, any fathers, founding or otherwise, who are even marginally responsible for our present angst-ridden condition.

My teenage life becomes dark and solitary. Riverside feels like a condition, a malaise with no cure. Riverside feels like forever. Were I literally chained up in jail, at least I would have tangible, identifiable bonds to strain against. But as I wander freely through Riverside streets, as the Santa Ana winds blow up, rattling palm fronds, creaking eucalyptus branches, blasting orange trees, making my heart clamor for something more intense and meaningful, I can't even identify what my bonds consist of. It sucks here. Somewhere—anywhere—else has to be an improvement. Strip Riverside away, peel it back like an orange skin, and I'll be left with what I covet, whatever that might be.

I imagine that if I were stuck in a cornfield somewhere in Iowa, I could always dream of the West. I could always imagine my escape to the promised land of California, but when you're already stuck there, in the promised land, and it isn't living up to its promises, just where do you go? And I don't even *belong* here. I'm not a Californian. I'm not even really an American. I still hold Soviet citizenship. I often imagine that everything that has happened to me in America is part of a dream, and one day when I wake up I'll be three years old, living on the fifth floor of a Soviet apartment building with a different set of grandparents, and Leonid Brezhnev will be my country's leader, and snow will be falling outside my window. And I will be home.

I become obsessed with going somewhere else and becoming someone else. I become bad at school, as bad as possible, which doesn't come easy. I take to wearing black, heavy metal–band T-shirts, ripped acid-washed jeans, and a long black trench coat. I hang out with smokers and stoners and kids who spend more time being truant than in a classroom. I fail my classes. I am proud of the Fs; they require real effort.

I stay out at night, going on beer runs and joyriding with bad boys in borrowed cars. We drive up and down narrow roads, the dark orange groves whooshing past, and then suddenly careen onto dirt roads, cutting the lights and moving much too fast through blackness, thick clouds of dust billowing behind us. We park and drink fast, tossing empty beer cans under trees, smashing bottles on standpipes, flicking burning cigarette butts at the foliage. Not once do I admit to any of the boys that these groves have anything to do with me, that I have walked here in the light of day, and that what we are doing is a desecration of a far greater magnitude than they can imagine. We come here only because this place is nowhere, nothing, a place of darkness, erasure, a place where minors drink stolen booze, a place to yell "fuck!" and dump trash, a place more nowhere than the nowhere of the rest of Riverside. It's not so much a place as a negation, a nothingness without people or houses or lights. I shotgun beers while secretly quaking with my own unspoken dread: the fear of meeting Grandpa swaggering down a row, out to run the wind machines on a freezing night, or to look for vandals. I picture him tomorrow morning discovering the smashed glass, the crushed Marlboro Red packs, the Keystone cans that have been slashed open at the bottom and poured down a throat in a single deluge. I picture him picking up my garbage.

And all of this is not enough. To complete my transformation, I must go somewhere else. Finally, I take the only action that seems possible, the only antidote for my condition: I run away from Riverside. I run away nearly two thousand miles to a place where no fifteen-year-old Californian girl in her right mind would ever choose to go, and that's precisely my point: I'm not in my right mind. With two boys and $850 in cash from my bank account—money from Grandpa that long ago I collected in a King Kong bank—I head to the Greyhound station and board a bus headed for Picayune, Mississippi. I don't have any idea what I will do after getting to Mississippi. The point is to get there—or rather, to get away from Riverside. During our drunken three-day odyssey, I am horrified when one of the boys—the one who somehow ends up being my boyfriend—tells me, in slurred speech, that when we get to Mississippi he wants to marry me so I can bear him a bouncing baby boy with blue eyes. It's then that I understand I've made no escape after all—quite the contrary—but I stay too drunk to care.

My escapade ends in drama befitting my desire for *something*. I'm apprehended by the Picayune police and thrown in jail due to my boyfriend's dime bag of pot that's in my backpack. And then my parents are summoned. Come get your juvenile-delinquent daughter, they're told, or we'll press charges and turn her over to the state. While I wait in jail, Grandpa comes to my parents' house to plan the logistics of my rescue. He cusses. He says, "She's not getting another red cent from me."

My dad comes to my rescue. We fly back to Ontario, California, where Grandpa is waiting in his Mustang to drive us home. He jams his foot on the pedal, flooding the engine with gas, taking the car up to ninety on the freeway. His jaw is clenched, his face florid with anger. "If she was my daughter," he tells my dad in a level voice, "I'd beat her within an inch of her life." My dad, looking nervous, says nothing, and Grandpa doesn't speak another word during the trip. I'm smug in the back seat, knowing I'm protected by the generation of Grandpa's sons who took the brunt of his anger full on. I can hate him and take his money. I'm not his. He can never lay a hand on me. And my dad is soft and passive, a reader, a thinker. He doesn't assert himself. He doesn't run an empire. He works as a crop estimator and would rather read history books and study dead languages than tell people what to do. He would rather rescue his daughter from jail than take a belt to her.

Still, my parents take steps. They ground me. They nail my windows shut and take away my shoes so I can't leave the house. They take my door off its hinges so I have no privacy. I refuse to go to school. I sit in my room and hear everything that's said in the living room. Grandpa and Bea are often there, participating in family summits about me. One day, I hear Grandpa say my name and the word *schizophrenic*. He believes I'm crazy like his daughter, the one in a mental hospital. It seems like such an easy out, a complete absolution of guilt. If I'm crazy, no one's to blame. If I'm crazy, everyone can stop trying to fix me. That he would give up on me, consigning me to the nuthouse, feels like a betrayal I will never forgive.

He gives me no more money. I'm not to be trusted, not with a single dime. Whenever my parents have to leave the house, he comes to baby-sit me. He sits in the living room, believing that I'm reading or listening to music in my room, blasting Bon Jovi or Aerosmith; meanwhile, the boys come to my window—which I've secretly pried open—and pass me bottles and joints. I get drunk and stoned while he sits out there, a dumb old man, an idiot.

❦

Riverside, California, circa 1979

Grandpa's in such a high mood that he swings through the drive-through at the Alta Dena Dairy to pick up a gallon of banana-nut ice cream on the way home. It's really his home, a large turn-of-the-century farmhouse that he bought for his big family—a wife and six kids—in the mid-1950s, but now I consider it my home, too. I barely even remember my first home, a cramped Soviet apartment. Home is here now, with Grandpa and Grandma Bea, with three of their grown sons, including my father, the eldest, who showed little interest in ranch work and who went to college and graduate school and then traveled to the Soviet Union.

Bea puts out plates of dinner on the Formica kitchen table—tuna casserole, fruit cocktail on a mound of cottage cheese, and peas—and I sit down with Grandpa to eat. The people in my family never all come together to eat at a table, not even on holidays. They eat in different places in the house, often at different times.

Grandpa reaches over and pulls a toothpick out of the toothpick cup.

"Let me teach you how to eat peas," he says, giving me a diabolical grin.

I watch him impale a pea on the end of his toothpick and stick it in his mouth. He stabs another and another. Soon, I am following suit, stabbing the peas and popping them into my mouth. Bea brings paper napkins to the table.

"Oh Bob, what are you teaching her that for?" she says, annoyed.

"What?!" Grandpa booms. "I'm just showing her how to eat peas!"

⚘

In my memory, he saves me. Or he tries to save me. But memory deceives, moving events around, erasing some and connecting others. In my memory, he hires me to paint the standpipes on the family groves, and he saves me. But when I look back at the records, I see that a full year passes between my Mississippi adventure and the painting of the standpipes. In the interim, I go back to high school and get five As and one A- on my sophomore report card. I have already saved myself. I have reinvented myself again; I'm now the smart girl with a past, the smart but wild and volatile girl. I'm the girl who's going to be a writer. When my mom shows Grandpa one of my poems printed in a magazine that showcases children's writing, he sits down to read the whole thing. "This is real good," he tells me. "You know, you could make more money writing by the time you're twenty-one than I've made in a lifetime." I write this down in my diary.

Other things happen. For the first time I get paid for my writing: thirty dollars for a poem. I start a paper route and get up at five every morning to deliver newspapers. I am earning my own cash. I have rehabilitated myself. And it is then—the summer after my sophomore year—that he hires me and Alex to paint the standpipes at his groves.

The two groves together, totaling twenty-five acres, have 2,503 trees that are irrigated by 187 standpipes, squat concrete posts that stick about a foot out of the ground, one for every row of trees. Connected to underground pipes, the standpipes have small sliding gates that regulate the amount of water coming out. Each standpipe is numbered. Our task is to clean each one, paint it all white, and then paint its number on top in black paint. It's simple, tedious work, yet I am stunned that he has asked me to do this. What could I ever do for the groves? Me, a mere girl? And Alex, who has only just turned eleven and who is turning out shy and bookish? For the first time, I suspect Grandpa of softness. I suspect he is doing me a special kindness, that his impulse to hire me comes from some vulnerable place.

Grandpa puts me in charge. I instruct Alex to clean the snails off the standpipes with a wire brush. We both slather on the white paint, but I do all the numbering myself. Grandpa brings me a set of metal house numbers, which I carefully trace in pencil on the fresh, white top of each standpipe. Then I carefully fill in the numeral with black paint on the end of a fine-tipped brush. We work for a week. Grandpa picks us up in the mornings, drops us at the groves, and then he leaves to do other work, reappearing at lunchtime with a McDonald's bag. I share fries with one of the stray cats that lives at the groves. Grandpa puts out old pie tins of cat food. He leaves us to work into the afternoon and takes us home at dinnertime.

He tells us, more than once, how plainly he'll be able to see the new, stark black numbers against the white. His vision is cloudy with cataracts; he needs those numbers big and bold. He says the paint will last fifteen or twenty years. He wants us to know our work will endure. He wants us to have pride in a job well done. Suddenly I feel closer to him than I have since early childhood. Finally he expects something of me. Finally his money is attached not to his whims but to my own work. This is different from the bills he hands out as tokens of love, buying affection. He pays us minimum wage, $4.25 an hour, for a forty-hour week.

How beautifully those brilliant white pipes with their crisp black numbers gleam among the green trees. I see, as we complete our work, that the reason for our toil is not just so I can have a little spending money, not just so Grandpa can spot the numbers easily. I can see that we are preserving the groves themselves, keeping them pristine, orange-crate worthy. We are protecting them from the encroachment of the future, of other landscapes. Because if they are beautiful, they must endure. If we keep them beautiful, if we protect them, we can save them. I'm certain Grandpa feels this, though he doesn't say it.

The day is hot and still. We paint and paint. The sun shines down on the dark canopies of the trees. Grandpa stands over us, not speaking. The standpipes seem to stretch forever. The day seems endless. Looking up at Grandpa, at his wide-legged stance, his big gut eclipsing the sun, his darkly shadowed face, I don't know what to think. I don't know what to feel. If he's glowering in disapproval, I don't know it. If he's beaming with pride, I don't know it. I have nothing to say. And even if I did, there is just so much time. Whatever is in my heart is not fully formed. Whatever I will have to say I don't yet have the words for. But I have my entire life. I am sixteen years old, and there is more time than I will ever know what to do with.

🌿

Riverside, California, circa 1979

I'm stabbing peas while Grandpa and Bea discuss furniture, something about the antique gold-leaf sofa that recently appeared in the house. I stand to get more peas, picking up my plate. Suddenly Grandpa opens up his mouth and lets loose a terrible roar. When he bellows again, I can just make out the words. "You like to spend money more than anyone I ever met!" This is directed at Bea. She stands with her lips pursed and says nothing. Their shared antagonism hangs in the air, thick and toxic like smog. I am still clinging to my plate, and now Grandpa and Bea both look at me.

"Honey, you're dropping your dinner," Bea says, coming toward me. I look down and see that I am holding the plate canted at an angle, and the tuna casserole has slid to the floor.

"Is that how you do things in Russia? Huh?!" Grandpa suddenly booms. "Do those Russians hold their plates sideways? Huh?!" Grandpa spurts out his wicked "hee hee hee hee hee" laugh while Bea helps me pick up my dinner. Grandpa continues to guffaw and mutter to himself, "That's how they do things in Russia." I stay near Bea.

"Oh, knock it off, Bob," she says quietly from the sink.

"Huh?!" he bellows.

I hang back, waiting for Grandpa to finish his dinner. I don't want his mood to sour, jeopardizing my chances for ice cream. Grandpa has five tall, strong sons and a movie star–beautiful wife, and they all fear him. I fear him too, but I'm willing to take certain risks for ice cream. Sometimes when he roars at one of his sons or at Bea, I'm so terrified that I can't hear his words. When he's angry, he's like a red-faced bull with a great tendoned neck, half blind and half deaf with rage. His unpredictability terrifies me. What might make him hee-haw one day will make him bellow the next. In fact, his guffaws and roars seem to spew from the same source. I imagine that there's a switch deep in his big gut somewhere that gets flipped back and forth from angry and yelling to amused and laughing on an arbitrary basis. Sometimes my antics are cute and comical, and sometimes they provoke bawling roars of "Knock it off!!" Behind his back, his sons call him the Duke, after John Wayne, due to the resemblance. I've never even heard any of his sons refer to him as "Dad" or "Father"; he's always the Duke. John Wayne has only recently died; he was just nine years older than Grandpa.

❦

The spring of his death is rainy and startlingly green. The air is clear, the mountains visible, day after day. I'm twenty-one and living in an apartment in Grand Terrace on land where orange groves once stood. The family groves are just a couple miles down the road. I drive past them every day in my new Honda Civic, which Grandpa helped me buy, giving me a hefty sum for a down payment just the year before.

At the end of January, I get a call: Grandpa's been hospitalized and is having surgery. It's colon cancer. I try to remember the last time I saw him, Christmas, and I realize that he was shrunken, withdrawn, his big gut deflated, while his grandchildren—my siblings and younger cousins—tore into the gifts from Bea, the cards of cash signed with his name in her hand.

I head to the hospital shortly after his surgery and find him in the ICU, unconscious, emaciated, his bare chest small, almost a boy's, with just a few sparse gray hairs around his nipples. He's never appeared shirtless in my presence, and immediately I see that my being here is an intrusion of his privacy. I turn and leave, and I never tell anyone that I have been here, that I have seen him like this. Driving back, I take my new car down Palmyrita, pushing the gas until the needle of the speedometer touches one hundred miles per hour, then easing off.

When he's conscious, I take Natasha with me to see him at the hospital. I want Grandpa to see that we are dutiful, caring granddaughters. I want to show him that though we are girls, our devotion is true. We visit a couple of times a week, and afterward I take Natasha driving. We drive all over the Inland Empire, trying to lose our way and become disoriented, but always eventually coming out in a place we know. We can't seem to lose ourselves. I drive most often the roads by the groves, looking at all those trees.

A dilapidated sofa is dumped on the edge of the road, and several nights later there's another, and still another. Soon half a dozen wrecked couches dot the sides of the roads, canted over in ditches by groves. Late in the night on Valentine's Day, I drive with Natasha down Palmyrita, and ahead of us we see a small fire glowing in the blackness. As we approach, we see that one of the couches is on fire, and my eyes tear up as I slow down and look at it, this blazing physical manifestation of my grief. Because my grieving, I realize, has already begun, even before death. But I can't say this to Natasha. All I can say to her is, "What are the chances that we would drive by at this very moment, right after someone lit that fire?"

He is lucid but weak, tiring easily. He is courteous, asking questions, seeming genuinely interested in the answers. He seems to want information about the world, about the exact circumstances he's leaving behind. He wants a vision of the future. I give him one.

"How's Jeff?" he asks.

"Fine," I tell him.

"You two will get married, won't you?"

"Yeah. Someday."

"That's good. How's college?"

"Fine."

"Getting straight As, I bet. You always were a smart one. Gonna be a writer?"

"Yeah, I guess."

"That takes some smarts."

I lie to him on his deathbed. The truth is I've just broken up with Jeff, the boy I dated for five years, and I'm flunking out of college. Once again, I'm in some kind of careening rebellion, but this time it's private. It has nothing to do with him or the rest of my family. I'm trying to figure out new ways of getting the hell out of here, ways that don't land me in jail, ways that don't involve being rescued by agents of my family. I'm living in an apartment with a cat and no furniture. The only thing I manage to do is go to work each day at the newspaper, where I have the late shift in the sports department processing box scores. Getting out of work at midnight, I drive and drive, past houses and strip malls and orange groves, driving for no reason at all except that I have a new car and I'm twenty-one and moving feels like getting somewhere. The only other thing I do is fill pages and pages in journals, which also feels like getting somewhere. I write:

I want to go in there and kick him and say, Dammit, old man! Fight! Live! What the fuck is wrong with you? How can you lose the will to live? How did you manage that? But instead I go in there and stare at him with sad eyes, ask him who sent which bouquet of flowers, if he's watched any TV, if he can eat solid foods. And he answers and asks if Bea gave us our allowance, how's school and the car and Jeff? I wish I could get into his head and swipe his memories before he dwindles away. I wish I could box them up and keep them. I wish I could see the groves and Box Springs and Palmyrita through the eyes of his memory. I wish I could know these places I love the way they were a long time ago.

The following month, in March, I write: *Snow-covered Mt. San Gorgonio, blue and white, rising between Blue Mountain and Box Springs, is one of the most breathtaking views I've ever seen. I love the mountains daily. I learn from them. I worship them. I look to them for answers. I look at them beseeching, demanding to know how to live. They soothe me. This is me and this is my home.*

I'll always long for this and if I leave I'll long to come back and if I come back it'll never be any better—no better than now, me, home.

At twenty-one, I don't know enough about him or about myself to say good-bye, but I know how to mourn him: by going to the groves, by looking at the mountains, by seeing the landscapes of his life. For the first time I realize that I love this land I have known for nearly my entire life; I realize that I have internalized it, that it is the landscape of my psyche. I yearn for more beauty, more mountains, more landscapes. On impulse during my vacation week I take Alex camping in Yosemite where we fill our days with hikes, with trees and mountains, while Grandpa continues his slow work of dying.

I don't believe in Grandpa's death, not fully, not until the very end. I believe it possible that he will raise himself up on his cowboy legs and come swaggering out, a veritable skeleton carried by the sheer force of his will. This seems more likely than the alternative—that there could ever be a world where he doesn't exist. I believe it is possible to keep on living if you put your mind to it, especially for a man as headstrong as Grandpa. I have never before seen death up close. My Russian grandfather died three years before, but being thousands of miles removed, I didn't witness his death. I don't understand the full force of death; it gets us all, even the mean and the bullheaded. If Grandpa dies, I believe that it will be a final terrible failing on his part. He will fail at staying alive—and just a month short of eighty.

He sees dying as a failing, too. He makes heroic efforts, more than once. When he's out of the hospital, he has one of his sons drive him up to the ranch to talk to his men. He forces himself to sit at the kitchen table and eat a grinder like a man. He tells Bea that he has to get well because it's his duty to take care of her to the end, to outlive her. It's part of his life's work. Leaving his work undone is unconscionable. But instead, Bea is the one caring for him. She puts her nursing training to use and becomes his hospice nurse, administering his morphine, keeping him clean, allowing him to be at home, to die in his own bed.

The last time I see him is Easter Sunday. I dread the lies I'll be forced to tell, but he's completely beyond questions now, out of his mind with pain, trying to recognize the faces at his bedside and to be momentarily lucid. "Hi, Grandpa," I say shyly, hanging back, not approaching, not touching him, and Grandpa says something—or tries to—but I don't know what it is. And then Bea hustles me out of the room, saying he gets tired out so easily, saying he needs his rest.

Several days later, sitting in my empty apartment, I get the call from my parents. Grandpa's dead. For so many years I thought that liberation is what I would feel at this moment, but that is all wrong. What I feel is an absence, a negation. I am not left with more. I am left with less. I call Bea and say, "I'm sorry to hear about Grandpa." And she talks, taking back the years of their antagonism. *He was a good provider*, she says. *He always did everything for his family. He never wanted to have to depend on his children or be a burden on his children. He was very strict. He was too critical of people. He was too hard on his children. We were together for so long I just took him for granted. He taught me to be frugal. He was up before five thirty every morning. He was a workaholic. In cold weather he'd go off to check the thermometers at two in the morning, even when he was old. He couldn't tolerate people being late. He was a tough man to work for or with. He expected from others what he expected of himself.*

She starts taking it back, and she will keep taking it back, for years, undoing the unkindness of word and feeling, recasting her image of him. For so long I have been on her side. And with him gone, suddenly there are no sides at all. There is a sense that there never was any enemy, that there was some profound misunderstanding. He has been utterly neutralized by death—not just neutralized, but transformed into someone else, into someone softer, a good provider, someone with forethought, someone who cared, in the end, about what would happen after his death. His family is provided for: his wife and his five sons and his daughter. Bea takes it all back, piece by piece over the years, until a decade later, she writes: *I grew to love him. I needed someone like him to keep me under control.*

I am guilty of revision, too. I overwrite him, in his death, his goneness. His life becomes a palimpsest. I can never write his life; I can only overwrite it. The harder I try, the more layers accrue, obscuring the truth of the life I want to illuminate. The harder I look, the less I see. The landscape that is his life becomes overlaid and buried by my very efforts to know it.

❧

Riverside, California, circa 1979
I sit with Grandpa as he watches the news. On his end of the couch the cushion is worn, the springs collapsed, the rounded hollow perfectly formed to his behind.

The fabric of his armrest is shiny with grime. He smokes and stares at the televi-
sion, digesting. I'm anticipating the ice cream, but it's not a thing you ask about.
I listen to his intestinal roilings. When he finishes his cigarette, he stubs it out in
a filthy ashtray the size of a dinner plate. Then he holds out his crooked finger to
me, instructing me to pull it, and of course I do though I don't want to, and we
execute the pull-my-finger gag perfectly as he lifts one of his haunches slightly off
the couch to release the jet of gas on cue.

"Bout time for some ice cream," he observes. With a great heave-ho he extracts
his behind from its groove in the couch and makes for the kitchen. Soon he shuffles
back in his bowlegged gait, bringing the whole gallon carton and two spoons. We
begin to eat. I take small, tentative scrapes off the frozen top, careful not to get
in Grandpa's way. Soon, though, we start in on our usual mission: eating a hole
through the center of the carton to the very bottom. Eating to the middle of the
world, I call it. We dig deeper and deeper. I fill my mouth with the cold ice cream.
I'm getting more aggressive in my work, taking larger spoonfuls, until suddenly
Grandpa barks at me, "That's enough!" I withdraw and sit there mutely, hold-
ing my spoon, watching Grandpa finish our work, watching him gorge himself.
When half the ice cream is gone from the carton, he puts the lid back on. Handing
me the carton and spoon, he says, "Go put that away."

⚜

In *Orange Empire: California and the Fruits of Eden*, Douglas Cazaux Sackman looks at the history of the region in terms of Frederick Jackson Turn-
er's ideas, exploring the history of the region "as a succession of landscapes,
each bearing the inscription of a dominant economic actor and activity,
and each written over by the next as if the land itself were a palimpsest."
Beginning with the horticultural landscape of indigenous peoples, Sackman delineates the distinct layers that followed: the Spanish era beginning
in the 1760s, the Mexican era in the 1820s, the frontier era in 1848, followed finally by the era of intensive horticulture that gave rise to the navel
orange. "The succession of landscapes from native gardeners to American
growers can be portrayed as an inevitable expression of progress, and it
often was," writes Sackman. Each landscape was viewed as an improvement on the one it overwrote, with the orange empire being the pinnacle
of achievement, the living embodiment of the American dream. And yet,
as Sackman points out, "instead of fulfilling a script authored by evolution
or destiny, these successions were in fact accomplished through a series

of 'human interventions' that could be called conquests." These successions, he continues, "involved a violent process of deterritorialization and reterritorializaiton." Sackman begins to open my eyes to the stories I have missed in my romance with navel country. As the fair-haired, blue-eyed granddaughter of the big boss, I knew close to nothing of the workers, the pickers and the packers, who made our life possible. The story of navel country is the one we—my white-skinned forebears—wrote, the one I am still writing. We are the colonizers. We are the storytellers.

Memory performs acts of conquest, too, holding a landscape in arrest. Writing about the intersections between landscape and memory in "When Nostalgia Is the Scent We Follow," Bruce Ballenger quotes Edward Casey: "Where one is can be determined by when one is." My Riverside—in its incarnation as navel country—is as much a time as a place. The landscape that I assumed for so long was natural—what could be more natural than a tree?—is artificial, man-made. The navel groves are arguably more a product of culture than nature. "The word *landscape*," writes Ballenger, "was used historically to describe a partial and often idealized view of the world on canvas or paper, a scene constrained by the edges and angles of a wooden frame"—or in the case of navel groves, by the borders of citrus-crate labels. And I do not see beyond the frame. I do not see the migrant laborers off to the side, up on ladders sweating in the sun with forty-pound orange sacks. Yes, I glimpsed them, but then I erased them from my mental landscape. Even the act of writing history is a process of colonizing the past. Revising history—looking to the Chinese and Mexican and other immigrant groups who provided the labor on which the navel empire was built—is a new colonization. Claiming my grandfather as my own territory to explore is an act of conquest. We colonize the dead. We perform interventions. The process is violent.

※

Riverside, California, circa 1979

I return to the couch because there's one more reward I can expect. "Oh, there was an old goat from Darby Town who had two horns of brass!" Grandpa bellows as I slip in beside him. "One grew out of its upper lip, and the other grew out of its—" He gives me a sly grin and then launches into a new ditty before finishing the old. "Oochie-koochie-kelamakoochie!" His songs are largely nonsense fragments, startling and disorienting. "Oh, you'll take the high road, and

I'll take the low road!" I smile at him demurely, as though in appreciation of his performance. This seems to prompt him to finally extract his wallet from his pocket—the reward I've been awaiting. He pulls out a dollar bill and hands it to me. "For my pretty little granddaughter," he says in a saccharine voice. I murmur a quiet thank-you. I don't have a firm concept of what money is good for, but I know he gives it to me when he's pleased with me—when I bring him the newspaper or when I wear a nice dress, or after he gets over being mad. I fold up my dollar and tiptoe across the room, slipping it through the slot in my gargantuan plastic King Kong bank. I pick up my Popeye-shaped PEZ candy dispenser from the table and return to the couch.

Grandpa opens his mouth and yawns. Even this simple action he performs like no one else I've ever known. "Whore house!" he bellows in the middle of his yawn. This is one of his eccentricities; it seems to be the only way he can get a yawn out properly. I profoundly misunderstand these violent ejaculations. I believe that he intends each yawn to be a beautiful performance, an aria, for in Russian the word whore—*or rather,* khor—*means choir, and so I believe that Grandpa is singing "choir house!" as an attempt to introduce grace and beauty into the mundane act of yawning. I wait, and the next one issues forth: "Whore house!" I believe he is trying to sing to me, and though his song sounds like the groanings of an old man, I admire what I believe to be his impetus for croaking out his music. "Whore house!"*

I watch him. Half a dozen whore-house yawns later, his head abruptly falls back, his mouth opens, and he begins to snore. I study him for several minutes, simultaneously amazed and appalled by his body. I look into his cavernous mouth, at his whitish-pink tongue, at his combination of teeth and dentures. I'm horrified by the wrinkles in his neck, his wheezy snore, the volley of burps and farts and grunts that issue out of him. I hold the PEZ dispenser tightly in my hand and stare into his mouth. Finally, I lift back Popeye's head and pull out a rectangular pink pill, which I lay gently on Grandpa's tongue. Your medicine, *I tell him silently.* Take your medicine. *His tongue rolls the pill around in his mouth while he sleeps. I watch it being churned and finally ground by his molars. Sometimes the pill disappears right down his black hatch, sometimes it gets tucked into a cheek, and once it just stayed on his tongue and dissolved. And once, I found a dead fly on the floor, and before I could stop myself, I put it in his mouth. He swallowed it right down. I have nightmares about that fly, about the deep black pit into which it vanished, and about the repercussions that I fear still await me.*

❦

As it turns out, my deathbed lies become truth—eventually. I do finish college and get married—but four years after Grandpa's death. And it's a different college, a different groom. Then I leave the Inland Empire again, heading to the East Coast and the Midwest, heading for unfamiliar landscapes, a life far removed from the remnants of navel country. Three states and five cities and eleven years removed from Riverside, I have the feeling that I'm not done moving, and that perhaps I'll never be done.

What happens after I move away is a series of endings.

On June 17, 2001, the National Orange packing house is consumed in a fire. According to news reports, about a thousand people stand outside that evening, watching what is believed to be Southern California's oldest continuously operating citrus-packing house burn to the ground. Arson is suspected, but no arrests are made. It's a poignant ending: if it happened in a novel, I'd never believe it. Real life, however, is not subject to the rules of verisimilitude. Truly, the whole thing goes up in flames. There's nothing left.

In late 2003, on a visit to Riverside, I walk in my family's groves for the last time. I don't know for sure it's the last time, but I know it might be. The window to sell is drawing near. I note that the paint on the standpipes is still holding up; they'll never be painted again. Walking in the late afternoon chill amid the trees with their perfect orange orbs, juice dripping from my frozen fingers as I devour navels, watching the blood-red sun sink behind the trees, I know that I have stepped, momentarily, into the dream. I walk in paradise tinged with melancholy, perhaps the only kind of paradise possible.

Two of my uncles, Ray and David, are now managing the groves. Many of the other groves that remain in the area have been essentially abandoned, weeds sprouting among rows of dying trees. In many cases maintaining the groves and picking the fruit is more costly than the fruit's market value. The newer plantings in Central California and foreign countries dominate the market. Our family groves, however, are never abandoned. My uncles believe that if they maintain the land and keep farming it, even if they don't make a profit, they'll have the upper hand. The value of the land will be apparent in its obvious fecundity.

I watch Ray work with a hoe, perfecting the furrows, his movements quick, frenetic. This is his life, too. He's dedicated his career to the citrus industry. I watch him maneuver an abandoned television to fill a depression on a bank where the soil is being washed away. He packs dirt around it, a temporary fix, just making use of the materials at hand. Everything has the feeling of being temporary now.

Driving back out of the groves, I notice another half dozen TVs left by the roadside. They seem to cohere, as if by a force of physical attraction. I am driving down the Avenue of Broken Televisions and Dying Orange Groves. I suddenly recall that Grandpa died in the spring of sofas, and now it's the winter of televisions.

Before I head back to graduate school in the east, my aunt Karen gives me some materials she's collected about the citrus industry, including an audiotape of an interview she conducted with Grandpa the same year I painted the standpipes. The voice on the tape is familiar, like the scent of orange blossoms, like the moppy heads of palm trees silhouetted against a smog-tinted sunset. There's a hint of Tennessee, a hint of stubbornness, but more than that, the voice seems to emanate from another century, with an impalpable quality that's more a marker of time than place.

When my dad came here in the '20s there was a lot of horses and mules being used and machinery that was horse drawn and stuff, and very few tractors, because I remember when they started making Colts and Caterpillars for grove work, cutting them down small. I remember when I was real young, it fascinated me, these tractors and everything. I could drive one when some of the mule skinners couldn't. "I'm not going to get on that thing," they'd say. I think they still had these horror stories of World War I in their mind, those big old tanks—they had pictures of them running over people and everything. And those Caterpillar tractors and Colt tractors—anything with tracks—looked vicious to them. It's just like today you're not going to get me on top of one of them goddamn rockets that go into outer space. That's dangerous!

Hearing his stories, I suddenly understand that his entire life is contained within the previous century. He is embedded within his time on the planet like an insect in amber. History has closed up around him, sealing him off in the past, and I can't budge him from his moment in the fossil record; I can't extract him from the landscape that made him. We are from a *when* just as surely as we are from a *where.*

He tells a rambling, anecdotal history of citrus. *I bought ten acres up in Highgrove in January of '48, and January of '49 that froze, and I found out real quick what it was to lose a crop of oranges that you'd worked all year for. In '60 they started planting in Central California. You'd sell out down by Disneyland for $20,000 an acre and take that $20,000 and go up there and plant ten acres for every acre you had here.* Here and there, bits of emotional truth glimmer through. *You see what I'm up against now. That's the reason it's a good thing you grow old and go on and let somebody else have it. It just upsets me awful.*

A farmer is the biggest gambler in the world—gambling on crops, gambling on price, gambling on cold or heat.

Bea and I, when we got married, we wanted thirty acres and our home, and we thought we would have one beautiful living. We had it for a while. We had it.

There are other tapes, interviews with the men who worked with Grandpa. Frank Garcia, the field foreman, describes how some years Grandpa would miss Christmas and New Year's because he was out with the men smudging and running wind machines. *He was square with everyone. He would tell them the truth. Sometimes he would let his own fruit fall on the ground. He didn't want to go out and pick his because other growers would say, "Oh, how come he's picking? 'Cause he's the big boss, picking his own fruit." And I would tell him, "Let's go get your fruit." "No, Frank," he says. "No, let's get the other ones first. It can wait." And then when we got to his, half of it was on the ground sometimes.* Another colleague, Dick Homiczewski, opens my eyes to another facet of Grandpa's character: the inferiority he felt due to his lack of formal education. *Bob would tend to demean himself in terms of his educational background or his intellect, his intelligence, and it was very unfair in my mind that he did that. I told him, "Bob, you know, your experience and your abilities go far beyond what you ever might learn in a classroom, in a textbook. You have an understanding of people. You have an understanding of fairness."* He also says: *When you've been involved in the business for that many years, those trees are a part of you. They're not just greenery out there; they're a part of you.*

I learn many things from the tapes. I learn that Grandpa's colleagues saw him as a morally upright man. I learn that he didn't blame growers for selling out. And I learn that he grew citrus not out of nostalgia, not out of a fondness for the good old days, but because it was his way of life. For him, it was the present, not the past. He knew the end was coming, and he wasn't sentimental. I am the sentimental one, finding it poetically fitting that the family groves are finally torn out the year my first child is born, the new generation arriving just as my family's old way of life becomes, finally, history.

❧

Riverside, California, circa 1979

I watch him sleep. Eventually, my mother will come find me to put me to bed, but she's busy with my baby sister. For now, I have Grandpa. His awful sawing snore goes on and on, relentlessly informing me how long and boring childhood can be, how eternal. With each raspy intake of his breath, I palpably experience time. Every minute is just a series of the rises and falls of an old man's chest. This is all there is. I watch him, vaguely repulsed, and I think about more ice cream and more money. I believe I know everything about him. I believe that for a trip to the groves, for obedience and demureness, I will get the things I want.

I don't wonder about the things I cannot see, the things I don't know: his private life, his tiredness. I don't know that when I go to sleep, when the whole house sleeps, the temperature will plummet, and he will heave himself out of bed to check the thermometers, run the wind machines, take care of his trees, protecting against one of his greatest enemies, cold. And the next day, when he's short of sleep and roaring at everyone in sight, when I don't get my trip to the ranch or my ice cream or my dollar, I will hate him a little for disappointing me, for being volatile and terrifying, for being a mystery I will never solve.

❧

In early 2011, twenty years after we painted the standpipes and fifteen years after Grandpa died, Alex and I set out to climb Sugarloaf with my two children. Weeks of torrential rainfall has swollen streams and deepened gullies. The hills have been reduced to mud, and here and there boulders have skidded down the hillsides, leaving muddy gouges in the earth. It hasn't rained like this since 1969, my uncle Ray tells me.

On the way up, Alex and I talk about coming here as kids. We tell stories about getting lost in the fog, about sliding down the hill in a downpour and arriving home covered in mud. Even though we are only in our thirties, our childhood feels like a long time ago. Maybe that's just the effect of having another generation present to hear our stories. For my children, they take on the quality of myth, stories of What Happened in the World before I Was Born, stories of What Happened in the Twentieth Century.

As I climb, the old citrus landscape burns fiercely in my mind. I imagine that when we reach the top all the orange groves will still be on the other side, unfurling across the land, and we will walk down and come out among trees. *This is my childhood,* I will say. *This, this, this,* pointing to each tree.

Summiting, I look down. My eyes find the straight line of Palmyrita, now flanked by warehouses and a tech park. I search the land for groves and finally spot the eight acres still being farmed by an elderly widow; the block of green is nearly lost in the sprawl of houses and the rectangular white roofs of warehouses, a new patchwork overlaying the land. I look a little farther, toward the base of Blue Mountain, where the family groves used to be. Here, there is nothing at all, just leveled dirt. The developers have razed the trees but put nothing in their place. The project was halted when the economy went sour, the developers running out of resources or vision, running out of some essential quality necessary to effect a transformation. What is here is emptiness, waiting to be overwritten, waiting for the next iteration of progress, the next conquest.

I try to think of a way to tell my daughter what this place looked like when I was a child: all those verdant nubs of trees tucked up against the hills, tidy as machine stitching, nature perfected. I want to redeem my grandfather and the land that made him. Before I can say anything, my daughter speaks. "California feels like home because we've moved so many times we always live somewhere different, but California always stays the same." This is her second trip up Sugarloaf so she has a reference point, a sense of continuity. "I can see why you would feel that way," I tell her. I don't say the rest out loud: *You have the disease of nostalgia, too, I fear. You will someday think back to your childhood when you mistook your own inno-cence for an innocence of the world, when you mistook the simplicity of a child's life for universal simplicity, your own happiness for universal happiness, when you mistook the long yawn of time that makes up childhood for permanence. Or worse, you'll believe that you just missed out on something. And you did. And so did I. And so did we all. Even Grandpa.*

Because when my grandfather arrived in California in 1922, even then people said the glory days were already past. I imagine the one perfect day—sometime in 1895 or perhaps 1905, when North and Tibbets were dead but my family was not yet on the scene—and it went by completely unnoticed. There was nothing remarkable about it, just a sun-drenched day with blossoms clustering tightly to the trees, their fragrance heavy in the air, and the Riversiders going about their business, driving their wagons up and down Victoria, men irrigating their groves, women buying eggs, and no one even suspecting that they had reached the pinnacle of their glory, that tomorrow and the day after and the day after the glory would slip a little further into the past, and even though more groves would be planted and more houses would be built, forever after there would be that sense of nostalgia, that sense that something beautiful and pure had slipped away. I see those Riversiders on their one perfect day, and they don't know it's perfect, and they have no one to tell them: *This is it. You're living the dream. Don't let it go by unnoticed. Put a border around it and paste it to an orange crate. Hold on to it, however you can.*

And then I picture myself as a sixteen-year-old girl, painting stand-pipes on a summer day that feels like it stretches forever, and I want to say the same things to her. I want to put a border around her. And does some future version of myself capture me here, today, at the top of a peak flanked by my young children, looking down on a vanished landscape, and does that future self long to put a border around this moment, render it as landscape? How many layers deep can nostalgia accrue? What is this palimpsest of the self? There is no extracting the self from landscape. We are the landscape, for it is our creation.

My children have lost interest in the scenery; they are climbing boulders with their uncle. A woman we've seen hiking from a distance comes up the trail, ascending the peak. She sees me looking at the view. She comes up beside me and looks, and we stand together just looking as if we'd arranged to meet here like this today.

"It's an abomination," she finally says, pointing at the landscape. "I remember when it was all orange groves, as far as you could see." She is perhaps in her sixties, my parents' age.

"So do I," I tell her.

She looks doubtful. I point to the leveled dry place, to the nothingness, and I tell her that my family's groves were there. I remember, I tell her. As best I can, I remember.

"It's an abomination," she repeats emphatically. I sense that her heart has colonized this place as navel country, too.

I want to tell her something more, something about my grandfather, but I don't know where to start. I could say that his mind, his psyche was filled with orange trees. I could say that I still wander among those trees, his life's work that has vanished, and one day I hope I will glimpse him there, the stern big boss, the duke of all this, the man to the end. In my mind I put him there, walking a grove on a freezing night, running the wind machines. I picture him caring for his groves while the world sleeps, the tenderness he lacks with people lavished on his trees, the depth of his love for this place as deep as the night. He is home.

Song of the Redwood Tree

I AM AMONG redwood trees because of you, a man who was never here, a man with whom I never inhabited the earth contemporaneously, the chasm between the year of your death and the year of my birth more than eight decades wide. And yet you've been a companion of mine since high school. I don't even remember when I first learned of your existence, when I first heard your words. It is your words that have brought me here, Walt Whitman.

Though we have driven among the trees for hours, abruptly we arrive, thrust out into unexpected chill. My five-year-old daughter stands shivering, damp and stripped to her underwear, in the stillness of a redwood grove while I work to remove vomit, the result of a big lunch and two hours of winding roads. This is not the introduction I envisioned.

My daughter stands ramrod straight, looking up. I wrap her in my fleece sweater, which hangs to her knees. I look around. In the misty late afternoon massive corrugated trunks unfurl like banners from the sky. They do not seem real. I am on the set of a movie. I think if I walk up to one and blow, it will sway and shimmer, revealing its artifice. I must convince my mind this is not artifice. There is a special quality to the light here I cannot name. There is stillness. This is a profound sense of coming to a place I have never been.

"They are too tall to see," my daughter says. And it is true. I look up, and I cannot see where they end. They vanish into sky.

You did not see these trees, but you wrote a poem about one of them in 1873, giving voice to a redwood being cut down. Your tree "abdicates" its place to a "superber race." How could you write such a poem? I have come here to discover the error of your ways, Walt Whitman. Your error, I think, was in never coming here.

Standing among these trees, the word for what I feel eludes me. Is it outrage? If it is outrage, you don't deserve it alone. The outrage should be directed at the entire Manifest-Destiny-westward-expansion-we-own-the-land project that's been underway since before the first glimmerings of nationhood. The outrage should be directed at myself, for living more than twenty years of my life in California and never being bothered to come see these trees. Now that I have children, I am bothered. Ten years after leaving California, I have returned to see trees that are so much a part of our national identity that my daughter has learned a song about them in her school half a country away.

❧

An elderly man bursts into the visitor center hollering, "I want to see a *really* big tree!" There is genuine urgency in his cry. We pause our leisurely browsing of postcards to watch him. He emanates a feeling that there is not much time left, for him or the trees. He is sprightly and enthusiastic, carefully listening to the ranger's directions, squinting at words on a map. He rushes out of the building with his tireless urgency. He's made it, just in the nick of time.

We've cut down over 95 percent of the *Sequoia sempervirens*, the coast redwoods, in under two centuries of logging. And the population we originally encountered was already a relict species, a fraction of the redwood forests that once spread across the earth. They have lived on our planet perhaps eighty times longer than we have. These vestiges of a former world grow very tall, and they live very long. The tallest known living trees are not quite 380 feet, though scientists estimate redwoods have the capacity to reach 425 feet or more. Some are two thousand years old.

The tree with the largest volume, I learn, has the mass of fifteen adult blue whales. Many redwoods are taller than the Statue of Liberty. These are trees that are measured in units of the earth's largest animals and mankind's great monuments. These are trees we cannot rightly imagine. They have been likened to cathedrals, places of worship. We gaze at them in awe, these giants from another time, in this sanctuary of their own making.

❧

"What is a tree?"

I asked my daughter this question when she was three years old. She chortled in exasperation. She pointed at examples in the world. We were surrounded by them. How could I not know what a tree is? How could I ask such a ludicrous question?

I wanted this most basic information from a child. I knew trees were deeply important to me, but my ideas were convoluted. A tree was a metaphor for everything in my life. It could mean all things. I could twist it to any purpose. I could whittle, carve, break, bulldoze, saw, snap, sand, rasp, and bend it until it took the form I required of it. I could make it into my own image. But I could not say what it was.

A child's metaphors are simple as she discovers the world, learns how things are the same. All big vehicles can be called trucks, all four-legged animals dogs, all good feelings love, all fears monsters. So what is a tree? I pressed her.

"Mom, a tree is a tree."

So true. A tree is already a basic category of existence. There is no further paring it down to its essence. It stands for itself. We are the ones who demand so much more of it. And it is both so much less and so much more than we hope and imagine.

You never saw California, Walt Whitman. You never stepped within a thousand miles of a living redwood tree. In the 1850s, the "Mother of the Forest" exhibit came to New York. The bark of a giant redwood had been removed at the trunk to a height of 116 feet, and these pieces were joined back together to create the exhibit. We have no record of your ever seeing the exhibit, but you might have. You were in the right place at the right time. You just might have gotten that close to a redwood.

Meanwhile, thousands of miles away, that tree stripped of its bark was dying.

But that was not the message of this touring tree skin. The message was: This is what our country produces. This is ours. Here is a symbol of our domination over these tallest, westernmost trees. This is progress. We have subdued it all. The entire shimmering continent is in our thrall. This is progress: this scalping of trees, this piecemeal hauling, this jigsaw puzzling of bark, this reassembling. Redwoods are too big to see; they are too big to move. But we want them for our own. I picture the men who skinned that tree as ants, crumb by crumb taking apart a cake left at a picnic. It is sweet, and they want it. This is all they know.

Maybe you never saw the pieced-together tree exhibit, but your vision was still piecemeal, a cobbling of what you heard and read. It is not outrage that I feel but disappointment. You disappoint me, Walt Whitman. I imagined a different poem, a paean to the redwood. To speak in the voice of a tree strikes me as a dangerous act of hubris. I cannot appropriate them, I cannot presume to know them so well, I cannot give them voice.

I hoped for more from you, the poet of democracy. But maybe that you created such a poem is just a symptom of our peculiar democracy, a symptom of a time and place. I am disappointed that your vision was not any clearer than your contemporaries', or, indeed, many of my contemporaries'. Maybe I ask too much of you. My own early twenty-first century sensibility will grow antiquated. How quaint and barbaric these words will seem; I write them nonetheless.

I am disappointed by your poem, but you were disappointed when you wrote it, weren't you? You had suffered a debilitating stroke and were partially paralyzed, convalescing in New Jersey. You were in your fifties, no longer the energetic, robust thirty-something who first challenged America with a new brand of poetry in 1855. Anytime we personify nature, anytime we give voice to it, our utterings are more about ourselves than nature. And you are that redwood tree in your poem, resigned to your fate, ready to sacrifice yourself for the future. But sacrificing oneself is not the same as sacrificing the trees. We should not confuse the two.

I am making excuses for you. I am fond of your kind, whiskered face, your American exuberance. Yet I cannot forgive you for so blithely "clearing the ground for broad humanity, the true America" in order "to build a grander future." An America that decimates its redwoods in the name of progress is not a true America. I want a grander future still.

If you could walk with us here among the redwoods, you would write a different poem. Of that I am certain.

❦

We look and look, but we do not see the trees. There is no place to stand to see an entire redwood. For hours we crane our necks, peering into the sky where the trees disappear from sight. We circle their behemoth trunks, stupefied. We are underwater. The light on the forest floor is murky, greenish, yet freighted with clarity. There is levity to our steps on the spongy duff. We are walking on the ocean floor. "The forest canopy is the earth's secret ocean," writes Richard Preston in *The Wild Trees*. Hundreds of feet above us, the trees collect fog from the air. Their canopies are like root systems reaching into the sky. They seem as distant as the stars from where we stand in our green-tinged seafloor environment. The trees reach into the earth and into heaven, drinking, drinking. We are blind to the work of the roots under our feet, to the slow constant pull, to the enormous suck, the seep of water upward, unceasing for centuries.

🌿

"You really can't tell much about what's happening in a forest from the ground," says noted redwood expert Steve Sillett in a 2009 National Geographic documentary titled *Climbing Redwood Giants*. So true. From the ground, we do not see the life that teems within the canopies hundreds of feet above us; we never glimpse, for example, the salamanders that live their whole lives in trees without once touching the ground. We do not see the epiphytes, fifty-plus species of mites, copepods, earthworms, bumblebees, huckleberries, lichens, voles, rhododendrons, currant and elderberry bushes, or the bonsai groves of California laurel, western hemlock, Douglas fir, tan oak, Sitka spruce, and buckthorn that perch atop the sprawling canopies that are like land masses held aloft in the sky. The canopies of the world's forests, I learn, contain half of nature's species. The scientists who rappel themselves into the trees, scaling redwood trunks like the faces of sheer cliffs, go into this undiscovered country. And they see.

Science has other ways of seeing. Researchers peer at the redwoods through microscopes, poring over cellulose, lichens, the structure of shrimp found snarled in trees hundreds of feet above sea level. They fly over the forests in twin-engine planes, using LIDAR, light detection and ranging, to create highly detailed maps of the topography of redwood forests, determining the heights of the tallest trees from the air. Dendrochronologists squint at great slabs of redwood cross sections, peering at the rings, counting, seeking out minute differences in annual growth. All of these are ways of seeing. And all ways glimpse only pieces of the whole.

❦

"What is a tree?"

I tried again, a year later.

"It's a big plant that's part hard brown and part soft green," my four-year-old daughter informed me. Her confidence seemed unshakable.

I considered challenging her: *always* hard and brown? *always* soft and green? But that wasn't my point. I wanted her to love trees more than I wanted her to be able to articulate a definition. I wanted her to pay attention to trees. I began to try to tell her why trees are amazing: they are living, they stay put all their lives, they give us the very air we breathe. She nodded her head, my words barely grazing her mind. This was no way to go about it.

❦

We come upon a titanic fallen redwood, its horizontal trunk like the hull of a drowned ship. Instead of being barnacled, its sides are lichened and mossed over. Instead of harboring darting schools of fish, the wood explodes with foliage, plants and trees shooting out of the top of the log, striving upward toward the distant canopy, toward light. Even horizontal, embedded in the earth, the log looms over our heads. This is the Dyerville Giant, which once stood close to 370 feet in height and was 17 feet across. On a Monday morning in March 1991, in the midst of a stormy season, the tree fell. This is a common way for redwoods to go. Most fall while they're still living; their most common natural threat is high winds.

According to Richard Preston, the Dyerville Giant's demise was reported on the AP newswire. It ripped open a crater forty feet across at its root base, and its root mass went thirty feet into the air. Nineteen years later, the roots that remain are like an enormous brown rose, withered, past its prime. My daughter gazes at it for a long time, saying nothing.

We look and look at the new life exploding from the tree's hull. This is what it has given itself over to. This is what it has made of itself in the past two decades. We walk from the brown earthy bloom of its root mass to where it tapers and gradually falls away to nothing, traversing its entire length. Finally we see an entire tree, from end to end. Or do we?

✻

"They don't translate into photographs," says National Geographic photographer Michael Nichols in *Climbing Redwood Giants*.

He spent weeks running a camera up on a pulley to capture images of a redwood tree, one grid piece at a time. His final composite photograph is made up of eighty-four separate images digitally stitched together—a patchwork quilt with no visible seams, a glossy color centerfold with four creases. For scale, the picture includes six human figures—one standing on the ground at the base, one beginning to ascend the trunk, another three perched in various branches about halfway up, and one resting in the crown—who look like Lilliputians scrambling over a sleeping, hulking, mysterious life form. We use technology to see what we cannot see: a whole tree. And the photo, frankly, is disappointing. It shows the tree without showing it. The photograph of the tree is not even as tall as my two-year-old son. It is a bonsai redwood, an exquisite miniature that's perfect in every detail. It is the entire tree, and it isn't.

✻

Ten years before I stood at the base of a redwood, I stood at the base of St. Vitus Cathedral in Prague, staring up at its towering Gothic presence, immovable, nearly sentient in its insistence on being. I scrambled around the bottom of that forbidding castle, looking at it from every angle, drinking *svařené víno* and coming back to look more, standing right up against its stone flanks, slanting my head this way and that, taking snapshots with my mind, jotting poems to it, picturing its origins deeply buried over a millennium in the past, its six-hundred-year construction, its coronations and funerals and parades, its stern Gothic face standing up against seasons, against sun and snow and wind and soft rain.

Now I stand with my body pressed against trees, looking up and trying to see them, these projects of creation that are centuries—even millennia—in the making. Even gone, a redwood can perpetuate. New sprouts rejuvenate around an old trunk or stump, forming a circle of trees, a coil of clones enclosing the ghost of its former self, a fairy ring. A cathedral, writes Richard Preston, is a "fairy ring that has grown old and vast, and has fallen partly into ruin." I look and look, searching these great edifices for clues about their existence—and my own.

❧

Merely seeing the trees is not enough, Walt Whitman.

"I saw them," said Ronald Reagan, back before he was ever president, back in the mid-sixties when he was running for governor of California and, by extension, governor of redwood trees. "There is nothing beautiful about them, just that they are a little higher than the others."

He also said, "I mean, if you've looked at a hundred thousand acres or so of trees—you know, a tree is a tree, how many more do you need to look at?"

I would say Reagan never saw a redwood tree. In the century that separates your words from his, we did not learn to see the trees.

❧

Like you, Walt Whitman, I am writing about redwood trees from the East Coast, looking west. In fact, I'm just a couple hundred miles from your home in Camden, New Jersey, where you wrote your poem. We peer across the continent, you and I, squinting to see those awe-inspiring trees. They're tall, but we can't quite see them from here, can we?

My son, who is not yet three, looks with me at images of redwoods in books. He asks me to show him the photos on my computer from my trip to the redwoods. He knows that I took his sister to see the trees, but I did not take him. He asks me if he will one day see the redwoods, too.

"Yes," I promise. "You will."

❧

Put your chin on the trunk of a redwood and look straight up. You will see the trunk ascending, disappearing before it ever reaches its conclusion. You will see the outer edges of the trunk as parallel lines appearing to meet at a point in the distance. I am jarringly transported to high school, to my unsettled, angry teenage self, itching to get away. I am sitting in a summer school geography class, drawing parallel lines that appear to meet in space and vehemently insisting to my teacher that if they *seem* to meet, then they *must* meet. I am walking the railroad tracks in the middle of the night, watching the silver gleam of rails unspooling before me in the moonlight, always meeting in the distance. I am watching the flat gray road with its twin yellow ribbons unfurl through the windshield of a Greyhound bus as I run away from home, fifteen years old and ready to start life anew. I seek those tapering lines of the tree, desiring it to take me somewhere away from myself. With my eyes I navigate its contours like a road to transcendence.

I look at the trees and think of roads, of the American sense of freedom. We can go anywhere; we own this continent by virtue, in great part, of our highways, and previously, our railroads. That there are drive-through redwood trees seems only appropriate. We don't have to get out of our cars for anything. We can drive through and satisfy all needs: fast food, banking, liquor, coffee, postal services, pharmacy, book returns, dairy products, scenery. We don't even need to be bothered about getting out of our cars to get married. By extension, a drive-through tree seems aptly American. Yet when I see one—complete with gift shop—I am mildly horrified. Do trees exist for our entertainment as quirky roadside attractions, novelties to drive through on our way to more important places, on our way to the rest of our lives? This ravishment of threading our machines through trees that seem to be nothing more than grotesque exhibits at the freak show called America is apparently worthy of a thousand kitschy tourist photos.

A drive-through tree strikes me as a heartbreaking symbol of our failings. We drive past without driving through.

❧

Like clouds, coastlines, mountain ranges, snowflakes, lightning, cauliflower, and blood vessels, redwood trees are fractals. Richard Preston explains: "The tree reiterates itself, making smaller and smaller copies of itself as it attempts to fill space and gather light. This is the mathematical form called the fractal. A fractal is a shape that echoes its own shape at smaller and smaller scales of size." If a tree is a fractal, maybe it's possible, in one sense, to see the whole tree while looking at just a small part of it. One tree, Ilúvatar, has 220 trunks that have been reiterated into six levels of hierarchy. "Ilúvatar is one of the most structurally complicated living organisms that have ever been discovered," writes Preston. Steve Sillett's sketches of the tree look, to an untrained eye, like an astrophysicist's notations about space-time continuums and wormholes in the universe.

And a redwood is like the universe, a big bang erupting from the miniscule matter of a seed the size of a flea, accelerating as it grows, supporting life, the worlds of lichens separating apart on branches like the stars drawing away from each other in the great gasping out of the universe, and parts of the tree growing back together and fusing like wormholes joining together distant parts of space. According to John Muir, "The clearest way into the Universe is through a forest wilderness." For a moment, these great trees seem rooted not just on the earth but in the universe.

And then, as we drive to another part of the forest, my daughter hums in the back seat. *This land is your land. This land is my land. This land was made for you and me.*

❧

Maybe I place more blame on you than you deserve. You didn't cut down a single redwood. You wrote predecimation; you wouldn't have sanctioned it. And yet your poem, in hindsight, seems a license to decimate. One tree abdicates. What about ten? What about a million? How many trees would you say need to abdicate their place until we've made the right amount of progress? When does our future become grand? Did you intend your song of the redwood tree to be a swan song?

❧

"What is a tree?"

I will ask my daughter again, nine months after our travels. She will not answer right away. Instead, she will go off alone to think it over and will return with a three-part definition. Thoughtful and newly self-conscious, she will be nearing six.

"It's part of nature, it protects you, and it's very beautiful," she will say shyly. She will have crafted her definition for my benefit, but I will hope also for her own.

And then we will go outside, and we will play a game in which we become trees. We will stand knee-deep in snow near white pines, holding our bodies very still.

"We are all trees," she will say.

"We are all trees," I will agree.

❧

My daughter stands inside a redwood tree. She enters the blackened fire cave cautiously, looking all around, until she is contained entirely within another living being. She will not know what this means until later. Whatever future unfurls before her will color her memories, her interpretations. I only hope that these trees take root in her mind and that they make up part of the patchwork of her memory. I hope that they stay with her and that her being becomes forged, in part, of trees. The trees are hers now. She has walked among these giants of the earth.

I turn on my camera and capture this: my daughter standing dazzled inside a tree. She is a wood sprite, a tiny creature cupped in the maw of a mighty tree, looking up into the blackened, hollowed depth of a redwood perhaps one hundred times taller and two hundred times older than she. She is standing perfectly still.

❊

"Do trees remember?"

My daughter asks this question shortly before we leave the redwoods. She wants to know, perhaps, if these ancient giants will remember that she once passed through here, an awe-filled juvenile creature of another species.

"They remember in their own way," I tell her. "They remember not with brains but in their very trunks and branches, in their very selves."

She stops and touches a tree, thoughtful. Their memory is incarnate in their physical being, I might add. Or, as Nalini M. Nadkarni writes in *Between Earth and Sky*, "The form of a tree is a frozen expression of its past environment and traumas."

"What do they remember?" my daughter presses.

"They remember wind," I say. "They are shaped by it. They remember drought and fire. They remember toxins and injury."

She nods. I could go on. They remember what humans have done. The "1954 benchmark" refers to the radioactive strontium that was absorbed by tree roots and incorporated into the living tissue of trees following nuclear testing. They remember, in their cores, the gradual accrual of years as growth rings. It is their written memories, the stories of their lives, hidden within them. Even at the level of DNA, they remember. As clones, each tree in a fairy ring has a perfect memory of every other.

We walk on, and she does not ask the question I dread: *will they remember me?*

No. Maybe. That she walked among these trees does not matter to the trees, except obliquely. Except that the children into whose care we will place the trees must know, as best they can, the staggering magnitude of the responsibility we pass on to them. She stops to feel the bark of another tree. She is only five. I say nothing more. The responsibility is a gradual accrual. It is years of looking at trees. It is more than words. The trees, I know, are more powerful, more lasting than my words. If words were enough, we would not have needed to come here. Every tree speaks. Every tree is a word. It utters what it is by being. I want my daughter to know this, but it is not something I can teach through telling. She must listen, with all her senses, to the language of the trees. She must touch the words with her hands and inhale their fragrance. She must live the words for herself.

❦

You believed in the potential of compost, debris, leaves-droppings. You knew that out of death came new life, that out of the fragments of history the present sprouted. "And as to you Life I reckon you are the leavings of many deaths," you wrote. All of America was your compost pile from which you plucked your poetry, and even your own writing was ground and churned, regrown, renourished with each subsequent edition of *Leaves of Grass*. You dismantled your poems and put them back together, rearranging the pieces, discarding some, using some to new purpose.

And in the end, you yourself became the compost. You bequeathed yourself to the dirt to grow from the grass you loved. You are like the Dyerville Giant, fallen but feeding new life. You tell me to look for you under my boot-soles, and I find you there, again and again. Your words are the compost from which this America has grown. Perhaps that was your greatest aim: to be broken down, ground up, reused, regenerated. You took me to the redwoods. You challenged me to see with my own eyes. I have used you to this purpose. And I will use you to others still.

The fall before we looked at redwoods, we raked leaves in Nebraska. We composted them, believing that something new would emerge from them, even if we weren't there to see it. Take note of these leaves, I told myself. Pay attention. There's no telling what they might become. Remember them. Let them live again in another form. The thick brown leaves of the pin oak and the light crisp ones of the silver maple filled our minds and topped off the compost pile so high that the leaves spilled into other times and places, into our redwood spring and our subsequent New England fall.

The pieces of my old life become compost for the future; these fragments that stay with me perpetuate, becoming the material of memory. The redwoods become compost for my new life in Connecticut. Bits of those tall trees come to me as I encounter new Northeastern trees. Seeing in pieces is the only way to see. We are not omniscient. We live in time. We see only so much. We think all is scattered pieces, and yet, "When we try to pick out anything by itself, we find it hitched to everything else in the universe," writes John Muir.

❦

You give me a multitude of words to live by, Walt Whitman, but for here and now I pick these words:

> There was a child went forth every day,
> And the first object he looked upon and received with wonder or
>   pity or love or dread, that object he became,
> And that object became part of him for the day or a certain part of
>   the day . . . . or for many years or stretching cycles of years.

So true. It is in the looking, Walt Whitman. We must look to our fullest capacity. We must look until we see. And even if we never see, we must still look. We must never cease looking.

I keep returning in my mind to the redwoods. I saw them in spring, and now it's fall. I'm in a new place, transplanted again. I look at the trees. On distant branches the leaves are starting to turn color, a dab here, there. Only the leaf tips of one branch are dipped in red, in yellow. One branch spangled in brash red seems to be looking to the future, trailblazing a path into deep fall.

Let me tell you about a child who goes forth. Every morning I point out the new red tinges on the leaves, redder than in any other place I have lived. We look together at these little fires in the trees. The fires spread. While his sister is at school, he looks at the flaming trees, and his eyes fill with wonder at the sight of his first New England autumn. He tests the air with the tip of his red tongue—and the trees, too, seem to be testing the air, reaching out their red tongues to the fall. It is that delicious. My eyes feast on the red. It is that delicious.

We walk and look at trees, he and I. I am teaching him to see the trees the best way I know how. I am teaching him, at least, to pay attention. What he sees in them is his own. And this looking, it turns out, is part of the song of the redwood tree. Its reach is mighty. It towers over the world. And so I show my son the trees. He looks and looks. And let us hope, Walt Whitman, that he sees.

Acknowledgments

"Living at Tree Line" appeared in the *North American Review*, March–April 2004.

"Soviet Trees" appeared in *Parcel*, Fall/Winter 2011.

"Cause of Death" appeared in *South Dakota Review*, Fall 2009.

"Lithodendron" appeared in *Blue Mesa Review*, Issue #26.

A version of "Translation: Perevod" appeared in *Witness*, Vol. XXII; an excerpt also appeared in *So to Speak*, Summer–Fall 2003.

"Quercus" appeared in *Alaska Quarterly Review*, Spring/Summer 2011; a condensed version of this essay, titled "The Wisdom of the Oak," also appeared in *Reader's Digest*, June/July 2011.

"Mulberry" appeared in *Adanna*, Issue #1.

"Navel Country" appeared in *Colorado Review*, Spring 2013.

"Song of the Redwood Tree" appeared in *South Dakota Review*, Spring–Summer 2011.

This book was designed and typeset by Lisa C. Tremaine.

The text and display faces are Adobe Caslon Pro, designed by Carol Twombly in 1990 and based on William Caslon's original designs from 1722.

Carol Twombly is an American calligrapher and type designer, and she is a graduate from Rhode Island School of Design, where her professor was Charles Bigelow. She joined the digital typography program at Stanford University, also under Bigelow. Working from the Bigelow & Holmes studio she designed Mirarae, which won her the 1984 Morisawa gold prize. Since 1988 she has been a staff designer at Adobe.